Se

G~~REAT~~
AMERICAN
STORIES 1

An ESL/EFL Reader

beginning-intermediate to intermediate levels

C.G. Draper

PRENTICE HALL REGENTS
Englewood Cliffs, New Jersey 07632

Library of Congress Cataloging-in-Publication Data

Draper, C. G.
    Great American stories : an ESL/EFL reader : beginning
-intermediate to intermediate levels / C. G. Draper.
        p.   cm.
    ISBN 0-13-364381-6
    1. English language – Textbooks for foreign speakers. 2. Short
stories, American – Adaptations. 3. Readers – United States.
I. Title.
PE1128.D675   1993
428.6'4 – dc20

                                                    92 - 14753
                                                          CIP

Acquisitions editor: Nancy Leonhardt
Production supervision, interior design
  and desktop composition: Noël Vreeland Carter
Desktop production supervision: Molly Pike Riccardi
  and Shari Toron
Cover design: Jayne Conte
Cover and interior art: Len Shalansky
Pre-press buyer: Ray Keating
Manufacturing buyer: Lori Bulwin
Scheduler: Leslie Coward

© 1993 by Prentice Hall Regents
Prentice-Hall, Inc.
A Paramount Communications Company
Englewood Cliffs, New Jersey 07632

Printed in the United States of America

10 9 8 7 6 5 4

0-13-364381-6

Prentice-Hall International (UK) Limited, *London*
Prentice-Hall of Australia Pty. Limited, *Sydney*
Prentice-Hall of Canada Inc. *Toronto*
Prentice-Hall Hispanoamericana, S.A., *Mexico*
Prentice-Hall of India Private Limited, *New Delhi*
Prentice-Hall of Japan, Inc. *Tokyo*
Simon & Schuster Asia Pte. Ltd., *Singapore*
Editora Prentice-Hall do Brasil, Ltda., *Rio de Janeiro*

CONTENTS

TO THE READER

This book starts at the beginning-intermediate level. It ends at the intermediate level. The first story in the book will be easy for you. The vocabulary list for the first four stories has 600 words. The list for the last four stories has 1,000 words. The longest sentences in the first story have 10 words. In the last stories, they have 18 words. There is new grammar in each story.

By working on this book, you will improve your
    reading
    speaking and discussion
    vocabulary
    knowledge of word forms
    writing

These stories were written many years ago by eight of America's most famous writers. You will read about the writers' lives before you read their stories. Special exercises will introduce you to the world of each story before you read it. And after each story you will find
    2 reading exercises
    2 vocabulary and word form exercises
    2 discussion and language activity exercises
    1 writing exercise
Good luck and good reading!

TO THE TEACHER

GREAT AMERICAN STORIES I consists of eight careful adaptations of famous stories by classic American writers and exercises on each story in reading skills, vocabulary, discussion, word forms, language activity, and writing. Prereading exercises introduce the student to the world of the story; and one of the prereading exercises in each lesson is based on a biographical paragraph about the story's author that appears on the story's title page.

The book is both graded and progressive—that is, the vocabulary, grammar, and internal structure of the stories increase in difficulty from the first story (which is at the beginning-intermediate level of proficiency) to the last (which is at the intermediate level). Structural, lexical, and sentence-length controls have been used throughout the book. The head-word list for the first four stories contains 600 words, while that used for the final four contains 1,000. Maximum sentence length increases from 10 words in the first story to 18 in the final four. New grammatical structures are added gradually, story by story. And words from outside the head-word lists are introduced in a context that makes their meaning clear; used again within the next 100 words of text; and then repeated at least three more times before the end of the story.

The exercises are so designed that the student must often return to the text to check comprehension or vocabulary. In addition, skimming and scanning exercises in the prereading sections often involve rereading of the writers' biographies. In short, an objective of the book is to involve the reader deeply in the text of each story and the world of its author, and, toward that end, to present exercises that are difficult if not impossible to complete without a thorough understanding of the text.

Finally, the book is designed for use either in or out of class—as a core reading text, ancillary text, or simply for pleasure reading. Its in-class use can take a number of different forms: teacher-student, student-student (pairs or small groups), student alone, or student-tutor.

C.G.D.

THE GIFT OF THE MAGI

Before You Read the Story . . .

1. *A Life*

   Read the paragraph about O. Henry on page 3. To you, what is the most interesting thing about his life?

2. *The Pictures*

   This story is "The Gift of the Magi." (MAY-jai) The word "Magi" means "wise men." The three kings on page 7 are the Magi. Each king is carrying a gift. What do you think these gifts are?

   Look at the pictures on page 5 and page 8. The same woman is in both pictures. Look at her face, her hair, and her clothes. What is the same? What is different?

   On page 8, the man is holding something in his hands. What is it?

3. *Thinking About It . . .*

   "The Gift of the Magi" happens at Christmas (December 25). In many countries, people give gifts at this time of year. At what other times of the year do people give gifts? When do you give gifts? Why do you give gifts?

4. *Scanning*

   Read the questions below. The answer to each question can be found in the paragraph about O. Henry on page 3. Read the paragraph quickly, looking for the information that will answer each question. You do not need to understand everything in the paragraph. But you must read carefully enough to find the answer to each question. This kind of reading to find information is called *scanning*. Try to answer each question in 30 seconds or less.

   a. In what town was O. Henry born?
   b. How old was he when he left school?
   c. Why did he go to prison?
   d. What is O. Henry famous for?
   e. What is *The Four Million?*
   f. How old was O. Henry when he died?

THE GIFT OF THE MAGI

adapted from the story by
O. HENRY

O. Henry's real name was William Sydney Porter. He was born in Greensboro, North Carolina, in 1862. He left school at the age of fifteen and worked in many different places. He also spent three years in prison because he took money from a bank. He started to write stories while he was in prison. O. Henry is famous for his stories with surprise endings. "The Gift of the Magi" is his most famous story. It is from the book *The Four Million*, stories about the everyday people of New York City. O. Henry died in 1910.

Della counted her money three times. She had only one dollar and eighty-seven cents. That was all. And tomorrow would be Christmas. What Christmas gift could she buy with only one dollar and eighty-seven cents? Della lay down on the old bed and cried and cried.

2 Let's leave Della alone for a while and look at her home. The chairs and tables were old and poor. Outside there was a mailbox without mail, and a door without a doorbell. The name on the door said MR. JAMES DILLINGHAM YOUNG—Della's dear husband Jim.

3 Della knew that Jim would be home soon. She dried her eyes and stood up. She looked in the mirror. She began to comb her hair for Jim. She felt very sad. She wanted to buy Jim a Christmas gift—something good. But what could she do with one dollar and eighty-seven cents? She combed her hair in the mirror and thought. Suddenly she had an idea.

4 Now, Jim and Della had only two treasures. One was Jim's gold watch. The other was Della's hair. It was long and brown, and fell down her back. Della looked in the mirror a little longer. Her eyes were sad, but then she smiled. She put on her old brown coat and her hat. She ran out of the house and down the street. She stopped in front of a door which said, MME. SOPHRONIE. HAIR OF ALL KINDS. Madame Sophronie was fat and seemed too white. The store was dark.

5 "Will you buy my hair?" Della asked.

6 "I buy hair," said Madame. "Take off your hat. Let's see your hair."

7 Della took off her hat. Her hair fell down like water. Mme. Sophronie lifted Della's hair with a heavy hand. "Twenty dollars," she said.

8 "Give me the money now!" said Della.

9 Ah! the next two hours flew past like summer wind. Della shopped in many stores for the right gift for Jim. Then she found it—a chain for his gold watch. It was a good chain, strong and expensive. Della knew the chain would make Jim happy. Jim had a cheap chain for his watch, but this chain was much better. It would look good with the gold watch. The chain cost twenty-one dollars. Della paid for the chain, and ran home with eighty-seven cents.

10 At seven o'clock Della made coffee and started to cook dinner. It was almost dinner time. Jim would be home soon. He was never late. Della heard Jim outside. She looked in the mirror again. "Oh! I hope Jim doesn't kill me!" Della smiled, but her eyes were wet. "But what could I do with only one dollar and eighty-seven cents?"

11 The door opened, and Jim came in and shut it. His face was thin and quiet. His coat was old, and he had no hat. He was only twenty-two. Jim stood still and looked at Della. He didn't speak. His eyes were strange. Della suddenly felt afraid. She did not understand him. She began to talk very fast. "Oh, Jim, dear, why do you look so strange? Don't look at me like that. I cut my hair and sold it. I wanted to buy you a Christmas gift. It will grow again— don't be angry. My hair grows very fast. Say 'Merry Christmas,' dear, and let's be happy. You don't know what I've got for you—it's beautiful."

12 "You cut your hair?" Jim spoke slowly.

13 "I cut it and sold it," Della answered. "Don't you like me now? I'm still me, aren't I?"

14 "You say that your hair is gone?" Jim asked again.

15 "Don't look for it, it's gone," Della said. "Be good to me, because it's Christmas. Shall we have dinner now, Jim?"

16 Jim seemed to wake up. He smiled. He took Della in his arms.

17 Let us leave them together for a while. They are happy, rich or poor. Do you know about the Magi? The Magi were wise men who brought Christmas gifts to the baby Jesus. But they could not give gifts like Jim's and

Della's. Perhaps you don't understand me now. But you will understand soon.

18 Jim took a small box out of his pocket. "I love your short hair, Della," he said. "I'm sorry I seemed strange. But if you open the box you will understand." Della opened the box. First she smiled, then suddenly she began to cry. In the box were two beautiful combs. Combs like those were made to hold up long hair. Della could see that the combs came from an expensive store. She never thought she

would have anything as beautiful! "Oh, Jim, they are beautiful! And my hair grows fast, you know. But wait! You must see your gift." Della gave Jim the chain. The chain was bright, like her eyes. "Isn't it a good one, Jim? I looked for it everywhere. You'll have to look at the time one hundred times daily, now. Give me your watch. I want to see them together."

19 Jim lay back on the bed. He put his hands under his head, and smiled. "Della," he said, "let's put the gifts

away. They are too good for us right now. I sold the watch to buy your combs. Come on, let's have dinner."

20 The Magi, as we said, were wise men—very wise men. They brought gifts to the baby Jesus. The Magi were wise, so their gifts were wise gifts. Perhaps Jim and Della do not seem wise. They lost the two great treasures of their house. But I want to tell you that they *were* wise. People like Jim and Della are always wiser than others. Everywhere they are wiser. They are the magi.

THE GIFT OF THE MAGI
EXERCISES

A. Understanding the Main Ideas

Answer the following questions with complete sentences.

1. Why did Della want to buy a gift for Jim?

2. Were Della and Jim rich? How do you know?

3. What were Jim's and Della's greatest treasures?

4. How did Della get enough money for Jim's gift?

5. How did Jim get enough money for Della's gift?

6. Who were the Magi, and what did they do?

7. Why does the writer think Della and Jim were wise?

B. Close Reading

If the sentence is true, write "T" next to it. If it is not true, write "F" for false. If the sentence is false, change one word and make it true.

1. ____ Della and Jim had a door without a doorbell.

2. ____ Della was very happy before Christmas.

3. ____ Madame Sophronie gave Della two dollars for her hair.

4. ____ Jim had an expensive chain for his watch.

5. _____ Jim was young, but his coat was old.

6. _____ Della laughed when Jim gave her the combs.

7. _____ Jim didn't show Della his watch.

C. Discussion

1. The writer, O. Henry, tells us that the Magi were wise. He also says that Jim and Della were wise. Why does he say this? Were they all wise in the same way? Do you agree with O. Henry?

2. A gift is one way of showing love. Do you think it is a very important way? Why or why not?

3. Do you give gifts to everyone you love? Do you ever give gifts to people you don't love? If so, why? If not, why not?

D. Vocabulary Practice

For each space in the sentences below, choose the best word from the following list:

| merry | watch | wise | |
| mirror | gift | count | treasures |

1. Della needed to _____ her money many times.

2. People say "_____ Christmas!" on December 25.

3. When Della looked in the _____, she saw her long hair.

4. Della's _____ to Jim was a chain for his watch.

5. Della's hair and Jim's watch were their two great _____.

6. At the beginning of the story, Jim has a cheap chain for his _____. At the end, he has no chain.

7. Jim's and Della's door had no _____.

8. Were Jim and Della _____ to give the gift of love?

E. Word Forms: Nouns and Adjectives

Put the correct form of the word on the left in the blank spaces on the right.

1. (sad / sadness) Della's _____ came from not having enough money to buy Jim a present. But she was not _____ to lose the great treasure of her hair. Why?

2. (wise / wisdom) People say that great _____ comes with great age. But I know children who are very _____, and old people who are not.

3. (happy / happiness) When she was _____, all the people around her were merry. Her _____ was like sun after a long rain.

4. (heavy / heaviness) The _____ of Della's hair surprised Madame Sophronie. "With hair this _____," she thought, "I will make a lot of money."

5. (expensive / expense) Cars are an _____ that John doesn't like to have. So he always buys old, cheap cars. But it is _____ to keep an old car on the road. So in the end he spends a lot of money on cars that he doesn't like.

F. Language Activity: Interview

What is your greatest treasure?
When did you get it?
How did you get it?

Why is it such a treasure to you?
Would you ever sell it?
Would you ever give it away?

Write down your answers to these questions. Then, ask two other people the same questions. Tell them about your own treasure, to help them understand what you want to learn. Write down their answers. Then tell your classmates what you learned from the people you talked with.

G. Writing: Madame Sophronie Speaks

In this exercise, you are Madame Sophronie. Answer each question below. Use complete sentences. When there are two questions together, join your answers using the words in parentheses.

Example:

What is your name? Do you have a store in the city, or in the country? (and)

My name is Madame Sophronie, and I have a store in the city.

1. Do you buy hair, or do you buy gold chains? Do you sell hair, too, or don't you? (and)
2. One day, did a young woman come into your store, or was it her husband?
3. Did she want to sell her hair, or buy it? Did you tell her to take her hat off, or to put it on? (and)
4. Was her hair beautiful, or ugly? Did you tell her that, or not? (but)
5. How much did you tell her you would pay?
6. Did she need the money, or didn't she? Did she take it, or not? (so)
7. Did you take her money, or did you take her hair? Did you want to buy it later, or sell it later? (because)

After you have answered the questions above, put your seven answers together into one paragraph. Then add another paragraph, about this:

Then a rich woman came into your store. She wanted to buy some hair. What did she say to you? What did you say to her? Did you show her the young woman's beautiful hair? Did she like it? How much did she pay for it?

LOVE OF LIFE \

Before You Read the Story...

1. *A Life*

Read the paragraph about Jack London, the writer, on page 15. Why do you think he wrote adventure stories?

2. *The Pictures*

Look closely at the pictures on pages **17, 19, 21, and 22.** Without reading the story, try to answer the questions below. If possible, do this exercise with a classmate, and report your answers to the class.

In the first picture, is one man walking away from the other, or toward him? Why is one man on the ground? Describe the man's clothes. What is he carrying? Where are the two men? Describe the land.

In the picture on page 19, the bones of an animal are on the ground. Why do you think the man is reaching for the bones?

In the picture on page 22, do you think the animal is friendly? Is the man in the picture sleeping, or dead?

In the picture on page 21, what does the man see in the distance? What does his face tell you?

3. *Thinking About It ...*

Tell your own story about the man in the four pictures. Use all four pictures in your story.

4. *Skimming*

Sometimes we want to have a general idea about a piece of writing before we read it carefully. This exercise will show you one way of doing that.

Read the first two sentences of each paragraph in "Love of Life." Take one minute (60 seconds) to do this. This kind of fast reading for the general idea is called *skimming*. Next, try to answer the following questions. Do not look back at the story to answer them.

a. How many men are in the story at the beginning?

b. Does the man hurt his foot or his hand?

c. Is the man hungry, or thirsty? Warm, or cold? Sick, or well?

d. Who finally finds the man? Is he alive, or is he dead?

14

LOVE
OF
LIFE

adapted from the story by
JACK LONDON

Jack London was born of a poor family in San Francisco, in 1876. He left school at fourteen, and became a sailor, a hunter, and an explorer. His first long trip was to Japan. When he was eighteen he returned to high school for one year. Then he went to the University of California at Berkeley. But again he left after one year and began to write seriously. In 1897 he went to the Klondike in Canada. Many men went there to find gold. London found adventures that he put into his most famous stories and novels. London continued to travel until a few years before his death in 1916.

Two men walked slowly through the low water of a river. They were alone in the cold, empty land. All they could see were stones and earth. It was fall, and the river ran cold over their feet. They carried blankets on their backs. They had guns, but no bullets; matches, but no food.

2 "I wish we had just two of those bullets we hid in the camp," said the first of the men. His voice was tired. The other man did not answer.

3 Suddenly the first man fell over a stone. He hurt his foot badly, and he cried out. He lay still for a moment, and then called: "Hey, Bill, I've hurt my foot." Bill didn't stop or look back. He walked out of the river and over the hill. The other man watched him. His eyes seemed like the eyes of a sick animal. He stood up. "Bill!" he cried again. But there was no answer. Bill kept walking.

4 "Bill!"

5 The man was alone in the empty land. His hands were cold, and he dropped his gun. He fought with his fear, and took his gun out of the water. He followed slowly after Bill. He tried to walk lightly on his bad foot.

6 He was alone, but he was not lost. He knew the way to their camp. There he would find food, bullets, and blankets. He must find them soon. Bill would wait for him there. Together they would go south to the Hudson Bay Company. They would find food there, and a warm fire. Home. The man had to believe that Bill would wait for him at the camp. If not, he would die. He thought about the food in the camp. And the food at the Hudson Bay Company. And the food he ate two days ago. He thought about food and he walked. After a while the man found some small berries to eat. The berries had no taste, and did not fill him. But he knew he must eat them.

7 In the evening he hit his foot on a stone and fell down He could not get up again. He lay still for a long

time. Later, he felt a little better and got up. He made a fire. He could cook only hot water, but he felt warmer. He dried his shoes by the fire. They had many holes. His feet had blood on them. His foot hurt badly. He put his foot in a piece of his blanket. Then he slept like a dead man.

8 He woke up because he heard an animal near him. He thought of meat and took his gun. But he had no bullets. The animal ran away. The man stood up and cried out. His foot was much worse this morning. He took out a small bag that was in his blanket. It was heavy—fifteen pounds. He didn't know if he could carry it. But he couldn't leave it behind. He had to take it with him. He had to be strong enough. He put it into his blanket again.

9 That day his hunger grew worse, worse than the hurt in his foot. Many times he wanted to lie down, but hunger made him go on. He saw a few birds. Once he tried to catch one, but it flew away. He felt tired and sick. He forgot to follow the way to the camp. In the afternoon he found some green plants. He ate them fast, like a horse. He saw a small fish in a river. He tried to catch it with his cup. But the fish swam away into a hole. The man cried like a baby, first quietly, then loudly. He cried alone in that empty world.

10 That night he made a fire again, and drank hot water. His blanket was wet, and his foot hurt. He could think only of his hunger. He woke up cold and sick. The earth and sky were gray. He got up and walked, he didn't know where. But the small bag was with him. The sun came out again, and he saw that he was lost. Was he too far north? He turned toward the east. His hunger was not so great, but he knew he was sick. He stopped often. He heard wolves, and knew that deer were near him. He believed he had one more bullet in his gun. It was still empty. The small bag became too heavy. The man opened the bag. It was full of small pieces of gold. He put half the gold in a piece of his blanket and left it on a rock. But he kept his gun. There were bullets in that camp.

11 Days passed, days of rain and cold. One day he came to the bones of a deer. There was no meat on the

bones. The man knew wolves must be near. He broke the bones and ate like an animal. Would he, too, be only bones tomorrow? And why not? This was life, he thought. Only life hurt. There was no hurt in death. To die was to sleep. Then why was he not ready to die? He could not see or feel. The hunger, too, was gone. But he walked and walked.

12 One morning he woke up beside a river. Sunlight was warm on his face. A sunny day, he thought. Perhaps he could find his way to the camp. His eyes followed the river. He could see far. The river emptied into the sea. He saw a ship on that silver sea. He shut his eyes. He knew there could be no ship, no seas, in this land. He heard a noise behind him, and turned back. A wolf, old and sick, was following him. I know *this* is real, he thought. He turned again, but the sea and the ship were still there. He didn't understand it. He tried to remember. What did the men at the Hudson Bay Company say about this land? Was he walking north, away from the camp, toward the sea? The man moved slowly toward the ship. He knew the sick wolf was following him. In the afternoon, he found more bones left by wolves. The bones of a man! Beside the bones was a small bag of gold, like his own. Ha! Bill carried his gold to the end, he thought. He would take Bill's gold to the ship. He would have the last laugh on Bill. His laughing sounded like the low cry of an animal. The wolf cried back to the man, and the man stopped laughing. How could he laugh about Bill's bones? He could not take Bill's gold. He left the gold near the bones.

13 The man was very sick, now. He walked more and more slowly. His blanket was gone. He lost his gold, then his gun, then his knife. Only the wolf stayed with him hour after hour. At last the man could go no further. He fell down. The wolf came close to him. It weakly bit his hand. The man hit the wolf and it went away. But it did not go far. It waited. The man waited. After many hours the wolf came back again. It was going to kill the man. But the man was ready. He held the wolf's mouth closed, and he got on top of the sick wolf. He held the animal still. Then he bit it with his last strength. He tasted the wolf's blood in his mouth.

Only love of life gave him enough strength. He held the wolf with his teeth and killed it. Later he fell on his back and slept.

14 The men on the ship saw a strange thing on the land. It did not walk. It was lying on the ground, and it moved slowly toward them—perhaps twenty feet an hour. The men went close to look at it. They could not believe it was a man.

15 Three weeks later the man felt better. He could tell them his story. But there was one strange thing. He could not believe there was enough food on the ship. The men told him there was a lot of food. But he only looked at them with fear. And slowly he began to grow fat. The men thought this was strange. They gave him less food, but still he grew larger and larger—each day he was fatter. Then one day they saw him put a lot of bread under his shirt. They looked in his bed, too, and saw bread under his blanket. The men understood, and left him alone.

LOVE OF LIFE
EXERCISES

A. Understanding the Main Ideas

Read the sentence (or sentences) from the story. Then answer the question about the sentence.

1. "Bill didn't stop or look back." (paragraph 3)
Who was Bill? Why do you think he didn't stop or look back?

2. "He took out a small bag that was in his blanket." (paragraph 8)
What was in this bag? Did the man keep it, or leave it? Why?

3. ". . . the fish swam away into a hole. The man cried like a baby, first quietly, then loudly." (paragraph 9)
Why did the man cry about losing the fish?

4. "He saw a ship on that silver sea." (paragraph 12)
Did he think the ship was real? Why, or why not? Was the ship real?

5. "But he only looked at them with fear." (paragraph 15)
Was the man safe on the ship? Did he have enough food to eat? Why was he still afraid?

6. "Love of Life."
This is the title of the story. What does it mean? How does the man show that he loves life?

B. Close Reading

Choose the right word to complete each sentence.

1. The man could not walk quickly because he hurt his
    a. back
    b. foot
    c. hand

2. The man wanted to find the camp because of the
    _____ there.

a. gold

b. water

c. bullets and food

3. One day the man found and ate the bones of a

a. deer

b. fish

c. wolf

4. The wolf could not kill the man because the wolf, too, was

a. hungry

b. thirsty

c. weak

5. The man found Bill's

a. hat and gloves

b. bones and gold

c. blanket and bullets

6. The men on the ship did not take the man's hidden

a. meat

b. blanket

c. bread

7. The men on the ship understood why the man was always

a. hungry

b. angry

c. laughing

C. Discussion

1. When the man finds Bill's gold, why does he laugh? Why does he stop laughing? Why does he leave the gold where he found it?

2. Do you know land that is "empty" — that has almost no people in it? Where is it? Describe it. Have you ever walked there? Did you like it? Would you like to live there?

D Vocabulary Practice (Antonyms)

Find a word in column A that means the OPPOSITE of a word in column B. (good-bad, big-little, etc.) Write the number of the word from column A next to the right word in column B.

A	B
1. weak	____ life
2. lost	____ open
3. laugh	____ full
4. death	____ thin
5. follow	____ cry
6. empty	____ loudly
7. quietly	____ strong
8. closed	____ found
9. fat	____ lead

E. Word Forms: Adjectives and Adverbs

Put the correct form of the words on the left in the blank spaces in the sentences on the right.

1. (slow/slowly) The man walked very _____. But the sick wolf was _____, too.

2. (sudden/suddenly) Bill had a _____ thought: "If I die _____, what will happen to my gold?"

3. (tired/tiredly) The man was hungry and _____. When he walked _____ onto the ship, the men there watched him without speaking.

4. (weak/weakly) The wolf was _____, like the man, and could only bite him _____.

5. (hungry/hungrily) The man ate the bones _____ like an animal. He was so _____ he could think only of food.

F. Language Activity: Riddles

For each sentence below, choose a word from the list which fits the sentence.

Example:

<u>bag</u>   He carried his gold in it.

bag	blanket	hunger	**camp**
strength	bullet	wolf	**bones**

1. _____ Without this little thing, he could not use the big thing he carried with him.

2. _____ He made pieces of it—one for his hurt foot, one for his gold.

3. _____ He killed it the way it wanted to kill him.

4. _____ He ate them, and he thought he might die and become them.

5. _____ He didn't want it, but every day he had more of it.

6. _____ He needed it, but every day he had less of it.

7. _____ It had everything he wanted, but he couldn't find it.

G. Writing A Letter Home

You are one of the men on the ship in "Love of Life." Write a letter to your family at home. Tell them the strange story of the man you found.

Where did you find him?
What did he look like on that first day?

Did you think he would live, or not?
On the ship, little by little, what happened to him?
And what was strange about him?
Why did he look at the other men with fear?
One day, what did you see him do?
What did you find in his bed?
Why, then, did you leave him alone?
What do you think will happen to him?

THE STORY OF AN HOUR

Before You Read the Story . . .

1. *A Life*

Read the paragraph about Kate Chopin on page 29. Look up the word "shocking" in the dictionary. Why were Chopin's stories almost forgotten until recently?

2. *The Pictures*

The same woman is in the pictures on page 31 and page 34. What is she feeling in the first picture? How has she changed in the second?

What do you think is happening in the picture on page 32?

3. *Thinking About It . . .*

"The Story of an Hour" is about a marriage more than a hundred years ago. Have marriages changed in the past 100 years? In what ways? In what ways have they not changed?

4. *Scanning Two Different Sources of Information*

For this exercise, use the paragraphs about Jack London, on page 15, and Kate Chopin, on page 29.

After you read each question below, quickly scan the paragraphs about the two writers. Find the answer to the question. You do not need to find any other information as you read. Try to do the exercise in less than three minutes.

a. Which writer was born earlier?
b. Which writer was born to a rich family?
c. Which writer started writing when young?
d. Which writer traveled a lot?
e. Which writer died later?
f. Which writer died older?

THE STORY OF AN HOUR

adapted from the story by
KATE CHOPIN

Kate Chopin was born in 1851 in St. Louis, Missouri. Her family was rich. She married, and had six children. She lived a family life like other rich ladies in those days. But she was well educated and liked to read and write. After her husband died, in 1883, she began to write stories. She wrote a book called *The Awakening*. This book, and many of her stories, shocked her readers at that time. She wrote about the freedom of women at a time when most women lived only for the family. Because the stories were so shocking, people did not read them for many years after her death in 1904. Now Kate Chopin's writing has been discovered again. People are interested in her life and work.

They knew that Louise Mallard had a weak heart. So they broke the bad news softly. Her husband, Brently, was dead.

2 "There was a train accident, Louise," said her sister Josephine, quietly.

3 Her husband's friend, Richards, stood with Josephine. Richards brought the news, but Josephine told the story. She spoke in broken sentences.

4 "Richards . . . was at the newspaper office. News of the accident came. Louise . . . Louise, Brently's name was on the list. Brently . . . was killed, Louise."

5 Louise did not hear the story coldly, like some women would. She could not close her mind or her heart to the news. Like a sudden storm, her tears broke out. She cried loudly in her sister's arms. Then, just as suddenly, the tears stopped. She went to her room alone. She wanted no one with her.

6 In front of the window stood an empty chair. She sat down and looked out the window. She was very tired after her tears. Her body felt cold, her mind and heart were empty.

7 Outside her window she could see the trees. The air smelled like spring rain. She could hear someone singing far away. Birds sang near the house. Blue sky showed between the clouds. She rested.

8 She sat quietly, but a few weak tears still fell. She had a young, strong face. But now her eyes showed nothing. She looked out the window at the blue sky. She was not thinking, or seeing. She was waiting.

9 There was something coming to her. She was waiting for it with fear. What was it? She did not know; she could not give it a name. But she felt it coming out from the sky. It reached her through the sound, the smell, the color of

the air.

10 Slowly she became excited. Her breath came fast, her heart beat faster. She began to see this thing. It wanted to find her and take her. She tried to fight against it. But she could not. Her mind was as weak as her two small white hands. Then she stopped fighting against it. A little word broke from her lips.

11 "Free," she said. "Free, free, free!" The emptiness and fear left her. Her eyes showed her excitement. Her heart beat fast, and the blood warmed her body. A sudden feeling of joy excited her.

12 She did not stop to ask if her joy was wrong. She saw her freedom clearly. She could not stop to think of smaller things.

13 She knew the tears would come again when she saw her husband's body. The kind hands, now dead and still. The loving face, now still and gray. But she looked into the future. She saw many long years to come that would belong to her alone. And now she opened her arms wide to those years in welcome.

14 There would be no one else to live for during those years. She would live for herself alone. There would be no strong mind above hers. Men and women always believe they can tell others what to do and how to think. Suddenly Louise understood that this was wrong. She could break away and be free of it.

15 And yet, she loved him—sometimes. Often she did not. What did love mean now? Now she understood that freedom is stronger than love.

16 "Free! Body and mind free!" she said again.

17 Her sister Josephine was waiting outside the door.

18. "Please open the door," Josephine cried. "You will make yourself sick. What are you doing in there, Louise? Please, please, let me in!"

19 "Go away. I am not sick." No, she was drinking in life through that open window.

20 She thought joyfully of all those days before her. Spring days, summer days. All kinds of days that would be her own. She began to hope life would be long. And just

yesterday, life seemed so long!

21 After a while she got up and opened the door. Her eyes were bright, her cheeks were red. She didn't know how strong and well she looked—so full of joy. They went downstairs, where Richards was waiting.

22 A man was opening the door. It was Brently Mallard. He was dirty, and tired. He carried a suitcase and an umbrella. He was not killed in the train accident. He didn't even know there was an accident. He was surprised at Josephine's sudden cry. He didn't understand why Richards moved suddenly between them, to hide Louise from her husband.

23 But Richards was too late.

24 When the doctors came, they said it was her weak heart. They said she died of joy—of joy that kills.

THE STORY OF AN HOUR
EXERCISES

A. Understanding the Main Ideas

Answer the following questions with complete sentences.

1. What news did Richards tell Louise?
2. How did Louise act when she first heard the news?
3. What was Louise waiting for?
4. Why did she feel joy?
5. When Brently came home, why was everyone surprised?
6. "They said she died of joy." Did she? If not, why not?

B. Close Reading

Choose one of the two words in parentheses to make a correct sentence.

1. Louise Mallard had a (sad / weak) heart.

2. They said (Brently / Richards) was killed in a train accident.

3. Sitting near the window, Louise was waiting to understand (her feelings / her husband).

4. At first, Louise (welcomed / fought against) the strange feeling that came to her.

5. She understood that freedom is (stronger / weaker) than love.

6. She knew she could live her life (with Josephine / alone).

7. After her husband died, she hoped that her life would be (short / long).

8. Richards tried to hide Louise from (Brently / Josephine).

C. Discussion

1. What does Louise discover about herself in this story?

2. Louise thinks, "Men and women always believe they can tell others what to do and how to think." Why do you think she believes this? Do you agree with her? How do people try to tell other people what to do and how to think?

3. What does Louise mean when she says, "Free, free!"? Free from what? Today, are women more free than men, or less free? Why?

D. Vocabulary Practice

Find words or phrases in the story that mean almost the same as the underlined words or phrases.

1. Chopin's stories made her readers feel *surprised and angry*. (See paragraph about Kate Chopin on page 29.)

2. She spoke in *short phrases*. (See paragraph 3.)

3. She couldn't *hide her thoughts and feelings*. (See paragraph 5.)

   4. She saw many long years ahead that would *be her own.*
   (See paragraph 13.)
   5. She was *enjoying* life. (See paragraph 19.)
   6. She thought *happily* of all those days *in front of* her.
   (See paragraph 20.)

E. Word Forms

Put the correct form of the word on the left in the blank
spaces in the sentences on the right.

   1. (broke / broken / brokenly) Josephine spoke
   _____ to Louise about Brently's death.
   She cried, too, when Louise's tears _____ out.
   Josephine thought Louise's heart was _____.
   2. (understand / understanding / understandingly)
   "Please open the door. You will make yourself sick!"
   Josephine said to her sister _____. But
   when Louise came out, Josephine couldn't _____
   why she looked so strong and well. Are you more
   _____ of Louise?
   3. (joy / joyful / joyfully) The _____ Louise
   felt surprised her. She spoke _____ to her
   sister, and lifted _____ eyes to Richards.

F. Language Activity: Class Project on the Role of Women

In pairs or groups, find examples of the role of women
today, as shown in magazines, newspapers, and television.
What do the "want-ads" (job advertisements) tell you?
What do advertisements for clothes tell you? What do
television programs about families tell you? Report to the
class on what you find

G. Writing: Josephine's Diary

You are Louise's sister, Josephine. Every day, you write in a diary. You write what happened every day, and how you feel about it. Now, you will write about what happened on the day Louise died.

Dear Diary,

Our friend Richards brought the saddest news today:_____

_____

_____.

After Louise heard about it, she_____

_____.

Then she_____

_____.

I was so worried about her! I called and called outside her door, and_____

_____.

I couldn't understand why she looked

_____

_____

_____.

We went downstairs to see Richards. Suddenly, the door opened and Brently_____

_____,

We couldn't understand what had happened. I_____, Richards_____, and Louise_____

_____. Later,

the doctors_____

_____.

I don't know what Brently thought. But I think

_____

_____

_____

_____

_____

THE TELL-TALE HEART

Before You Read the Story . . .

1. *A Life*

   Read the paragraph about Edgar Allan Poe on page 41. Was Poe's life an unhappy one?

   What does the word "detective" mean? the word "horror?"

   A "tale" is a story. What does the title mean: "The Tell-Tale Heart?"

2. *The Pictures*

   Look at the picture on page 43. What word can you use to describe the man's face? There is a light shining on the man's face. Where is the light coming from? What is the other man holding?

   There are three policemen in the picture on page 47. What words can you use to describe their faces? Who are they looking at?

3. *Thinking About It . . .*

   What do you think small children are most afraid of? The dark? Large, strange animals? Sudden, loud noises? Things they do not understand? Are older people afraid of the same things? Do most people talk easily about their fears?

4. *Skimming*

   Take 60 seconds to skim "The Tell-Tale Heart." (Quickly read the first two or three sentences of each paragraph.)

   Do not look back at the story. Look at the three groups of words below. Which group fits the general idea you got from skimming the story—group **A**, **B**, or **C**?

A	**B**	**C**
machine	flower	house
tomorrow	today	yesterday
study	enjoy	kill
new	young	old
thinking	happy	mad
noon	morning	midnight

THE TELL-TALE HEART

adapted from the story by
EDGAR ALLAN POE

Edgar Allan Poe was born in 1809 in Boston, Massachusetts. He is one of America's most important and famous writers. Poe's parents died when he was a child. He was raised by people named Allan. They were rich, but Poe was poor all his life. He lost several jobs because he drank too much. People remember Poe for his poetry, for his detective stories, and for his horror stories like "The Tell-Tale Heart." Poe died unhappily at the age of forty, in 1849.

True! Nervous. I was nervous then and I am nervous now. But why do you say that I am mad? Nothing was wrong with me. I could see very well. I could smell. I could touch. Yes, my friend, and I could hear. I could hear all things in the skies and in the earth. So why do you think that I am mad? Listen. I will tell you the story. I will speak quietly. You will understand everything. Listen!

2 Why did I want to kill the old man? Ah, this is very difficult. I liked the old man. No, I loved him! He never hurt me. He was always kind to me. I didn't need his gold; no, I didn't want that. I think it was his eye—yes, it was this! He had the eye of a bird. It was a cold, light-blue eye—a horrible eye. I feared it. Sometimes I tried to look at it. But then my blood ran cold. So, after many weeks, I knew I must kill the old man. His horrible eye must not live. Do you understand?

3 Now here is the point. You think that I am mad. Madmen know nothing. But I? I was careful. Oh, I was very careful. *Careful*, you see? For one long week, I was very kind to the old man. But every night, at midnight, I opened his door slowly, carefully. I had a lantern with me. Inside the lantern there was a light. But the sides of the lantern hid the light. So, first I put the dark lantern through the open door. Then I put my head in the room. I put it in slowly, very slowly. I didn't want to wake the old man. Ha! Would a madman be careful, like that? There was no noise, not a sound. I opened the lantern carefully—very carefully—and slowly. A thin light fell upon the old man's eye. I held it there. I held it there for a long time. And I did this every night for seven nights. But always the eye was closed. And so I could not do my work. I was not angry at the old man, you see. I was angry only at his horrible eye. And every morning I went into his room happily. I was friendly with him. I asked about his night. Did he sleep well? Was he all

right? And so, you see, he knew nothing.

4 On the eighth night, I was more careful than before. I know you don't believe me, but it is true. The clock's hand moved more quickly than my hand. I opened the door slowly. I put the lantern in the room. The old man moved suddenly in his bed. But I did not go back. The room was very dark. I knew he could not see me. I put my head in the room. I began to open the lantern, but my hand hit the side. It made a loud noise.

5 The old man sat up quickly in bed. "Who's there?" he cried.

6 I stood still and said nothing. For one long hour I did not move a finger. And he did not lie down. He sat in his bed. He listened. I knew his fear!

7 And soon I heard another sound. It came from the old man. It was a horrible sound, the sound of fear! I knew that sound well. Often, at night, I too have made that sound. What was in the room? The old man didn't know. He didn't want to know. But he knew that he was in danger. Ah, yes, he knew!

8 And now I began to open the lantern. I opened it just a little. A small thin light fell upon the horrible blue eye.

9 It was open—wide, wide open. I could not see the old man's face or body. But I saw the eye very well. The horrible bird's eye. My blood ran cold. At the same time, anger began to grow inside me.

10 And now, haven't I told you that I could hear everything? Now a low, quick sound came to my ears. It was like the sound of a small wooden clock. I knew *that* sound well, too. It was the beating of the old man's heart!

11 My fear and anger grew. But I did not move. I stood still. I held the light on the old man's eye. And the beating of the heart grew. It became quicker and quicker, and louder and louder every second! I knew that his fear was very great. *Louder*, do you hear? I have told you that I am nervous. And this is true. My fear was like the old man's. But I did not move. I held the light on his eye. But the beating grew louder, LOUDER! And now a new fear came to

me. Someone in the next house would hear! The old man must die! This was his hour! With a loud cry, I opened the lantern wide. I ran into the room! The old man cried loudly once—once only. His fear, his fear killed him! In a secönd I pulled him from the bed. He lay still. I smiled a little. Everything was all right. For some minutes, I heard his heart beat softly. Then it stopped. I put my hand on his body. He was cold. He was like a stone. The old man was dead. His eye would never look upon me again!

12 And now I was very, very careful. I worked quickly but quietly. I used a good, new knife. I cut off the old man's arms and legs and head. Then I took three boards from the floor of the room. I put everything below the floor. Then I put the boards in their place again. I cleaned the floor. There was no blood. Nothing was wrong. I was *careful,* you see? Ha! Can you still think that I am mad?

13 I finished. It was four o'clock—still dark as midnight. Suddenly there was a beating on the door. Someone was there. But I went down with a happy heart. I had nothing to fear. Nothing.

14 Three policemen came into the house. They said that someone in the next house heard a cry. Was something wrong? Was everyone all right?

15 "Of course," I said. "Please come in." I was not nervous. I smiled at the men. I told them that the old man was in another town. I said he was with his sister. I showed them his money, his gold. Everything was there, in its place.

16 I brought chairs. I asked the men to sit. I sat, too. I sat on the boards over the dead man's body! I talked easily. The policemen smiled.

17 But after some minutes I became tired. Perhaps I was a little nervous. There was a low sound in my head, in my ears. I didn't like it. I talked more loudly, more angrily. Then suddenly I understood. The sound was not in my head or in my ears. It was there in the room!

18 Now I know that I became *very* nervous. *It was a low quick sound. It sounded like a small wooden clock!* My eyes opened wide. Could the policemen hear it? I talked in a louder voice. But the noise did not stop. It grew! I stood up

and talked angrily, dangerously. I walked across the floor and back again. Why wouldn't the men leave? There was a storm inside my head! And still the noise became louder—LOUDER—LOUDER! I beat my hands on the table. I said dangerous things in a loud voice. But still the men talked happily and smiled. Couldn't they hear? Was it possible? Oh, God! No, no! They heard! They knew! They laughed at my hopes, and smiled at my fears. I knew it then and I know it now. I couldn't keep still! Anything was better than their smiles and laughing! And now—again!—listen! louder! LOUDER! LOUDER!

19 "Stop!" I cried. "Enough! Enough! Pull up the boards! Below the floor! Here, here!—It is the beating of his horrible heart!"

THE TELL-TALE HEART
EXERCISES

A. Understanding the Main Ideas: Cause and Effect

Complete each sentence below by choosing **a**, **b**, or **c**. The first half of each sentence tells about something that happened in the story (*the effect*). The second half should tell why it happened (*the cause*).

1. The young man wanted to kill the old man because
  a. he loved the old man.
  b. he didn't like the old man's eye.
  c. he wanted the old man's gold.
2. He opened the old man's door carefully because
  a. the old man was mad.
  b. he thought the old man was horrible.
  c. he didn't want to wake the old man.
3. Every morning the young man was friendly because
  a. he held a thin light over the old man's eye.

   b. he didn't want the old man to think anything was wrong

   c. he was angry at the old man.

4. The police came to the house because

   a. someone in the next house heard a cry.

   b. they knew the young man was mad.

   c. they wanted to sit, talk, and laugh.

5. The young man talked louder and louder to the police because

   a. they couldn't hear him.

   b. he thought they would hear the beating of the old man's heart.

   c. he was very angry at them.

6. The young man killed the old man and then told the police because

   a. they all laughed and smiled at him.

   b. the old man's heart beat louder and louder.

   c. the young man was mad.

B. Close Reading

Read the first half of a sentence in column A. Then draw a line from it to the second half in column B that best completes the meaning. The first one is done for you.

A	**B**
1. The madman thought	when he heard a low, quick sound
2. He wanted to kill the old man	after the young man ran into the room
3. The old man woke up	that he could hear all things in the earth and in the sky

4. The old man died	when the young man's hand hit the lantern
5. The young man told the police	because he was afraid of the beating of the heart below the floor
6. The young man became nervous	that the old man was in another town
7. He told the police about the killing	because he hated his cold blue eye

C. Discussion

1. The old man was dead. His body, in pieces, was below the floor. But the young man believed that he could hear the old man's heart beating. Why?
2. What do you think will happen to the man after the police take him away? Should he go to prison? To a doctor? Should he be killed?
3. Do you enjoy horror stories? Do you enjoy horror movies? Why, or why not?

D. Vocabulary Practice: Words for Unpleasant People and Things

Choose the word below that best completes the description of the person or thing in the sentences that follow:

mad   horrible   angry   fear   danger   nervous

1. The young man couldn't sit still. He talked quickly, loudly. His eyes moved all over the room. His hands

shook. He was very _____.

2. The eye was cold, light blue, the eye of a bird. His blood ran cold when he looked at it. He thought the eye was _____.

3. He killed the old man, cut him in pieces, and put the pieces below the floor. But he believed that the old man's heart was still beating. Surely he was

_____.

4. When the policemen came, he took them into the old man's room. He sat on the boards over the dead man's body. He tried to talk easily. But truly he was in

_____.

5. He said he loved the old man. The old man was kind to him. The old man never hurt him. It was only the old man's eye that made him so _____.

6. What really killed the old man? It wasn't a knife. It wasn't even the open lantern, or the young man's loud cry. It was his own _____.

E. Word Forms: Adjective or Adverb?

Put the correct form of the word on the left in the blank space in the sentence.

1. (horrible / horribly) The old man's eye seemed _____ to the young man.

2. (careful / carefully) He didn't want to make any noise, so he opened the lantern _____.

3. (dangerous / dangerously) The police thought the young man might be _____, so they were careful in the way they spoke to him.

4. (quick / quickly) The heart beat _____.

F. Language Activity: The Police

Choose one of the following activities. Prepare to speak about your topic to a classmate, a small group, or the entire class.

1. Find and read a newspaper or magazine article about police activity.
2. Talk about the role of the police in a t.v. program or movie you have seen recently.
3. Talk to a policeman or policewoman about his or her job.
4. In an encyclopedia, read about the history of the police.

G. Writing: A Police Report

You are one of the policemen in "The Tell-Tale Heart." You must write a report about the killing. In your report, you should answer some or all of the following questions:

What time was it when you went to the young man's house?
Why did you go there?
Did he meet you at the door?
How did he seem — friendly? Nervous? Angry?
Did he ask you to come in?
Did you ask about the old man?
What did he say about the old man?
Where did he take you?
Did he ask you to sit, or to stand?

Did he sit or stand?
How did he talk?
After some minutes of this, how did he seem?
How did he talk then?
Finally, what did he say?
What did you find below the boards?
What happened then?

A CUB-PILOT'S EDUCATION

Before You Read the Story . . .

1. *A Life*

Read the paragraph about Mark Twain on page 55. What are his most famous books about?

2. *The Pictures*

Look at the picture on page 57. It is a picture of a steamboat. In the 19th century, these boats traveled on the Mississippi River, the longest river in the United States. The steamboats were large. Can you tell why these boats were important?

In the picture on page 58, what is the boy doing? Where would he be doing this in the picture on page 62?

3. *Thinking About It . . .*

A pilot is someone who drives (or steers) a boat or plane. A cub-pilot is a young person who is learning to be a pilot. He watches the pilot at his job. Then he tries to do the job. Do you think this is a good way for a young person to learn?

4. *Scanning for Specific Information*

Sometimes we scan a piece of writing to find one or two pieces of information. We don't read everything. We don't even need to get a general idea about the piece of writing. We need only the information.

We do this by reading very quickly. Our eyes move across and down the page, looking for a single word or number. When we find it, we stop and read more carefully.

In this exercise, you will try to answer the questions below by scanning a page of the story "A Cub-Pilot's Education." The answer to each question can be found on the page given. In front of each question is an underlined word or phrase. Let your eyes move quickly across and down the page. When they find the underlined name or number, stop. Read more carefully, and find the answer to the question. Try to answer each question in 30 seconds or less.

a. page 56 <u>Keokuk</u> Did the steamboat come up-river or down river from Keokuk?

b. page 56 <u>New Orleans</u> How old was the boy when he ran away to New Orleans?

c. page 59 <u>Twelve-Mile Point</u> Was the boy interested in Twelve-Mile Point?

d. page 61 <u>Apple Bend</u> Did the boy know the shape of Apple Bend?

e. page 62 <u>Island 66</u> Was the bend there easy, or difficult?

A CUB-PILOT'S EDUCATION

adapted from the story by
MARK TWAIN

Mark Twain's real name was Samuel Langhorne Clemens. He was born in 1835 in Missouri. As a boy, he lived in a small town on the Mississippi River. His most famous books, *The Adventures of Tom Sawyer* and *The Adventures of Huckleberry Finn*, are about boyhood and the Mississippi. Because of these books, Mark Twain became America's most famous and best-loved writer. He died in 1910 at the age of seventy-five. The following story is from his book *Life on the Mississippi*.

I

All the boys in my village wanted to be the same thing: a steamboat pilot. Our village lay on the great Mississippi River. Once a day, at noon, a steamboat came up from St. Louis. Later, at one o'clock, another came down from Keokuk. Before these hours, the day was full and bright with waiting. After them, the day was a dead and empty thing.

2 I can see that old time now. The white town sleeps in the morning sun. The streets are empty. Some animals walk near the buildings. The waters of the Mississippi are quiet and still. A man who has drunk too much lies peacefully near the river. Other men sit outside their stores in chairs. They look at the town and don't talk much.

3 Then a worker cries, "S-t-e-a-m-boat coming!" And everything changes! The man who has drunk too much gets up and runs. Suddenly the streets are full. Men, women, and children run to the steamboat landing. The animals make a hundred different noises. The town wakes up!

4 The steamboat that comes toward the town is long and pretty. Her big wheel turns and turns. Everybody looks at her and at the men who live on her. The pilot stands tallest, the center of everything, the king. Slowly the steamboat comes to the landing. Men take things off the boat and bring other things on. In ten minutes she is gone again. The town goes back to sleep. But the boys of the town remember the boat. They remember the pilot. And they don't forget.

5 I was fifteen then, and I ran away from home. I went to New Orleans. There I met a pilot named Mr. Bixby. I said I wanted to be his cub-pilot, or learner. He said no—but only once. I said yes a hundred times. So in the end I won. He said he would teach me the river. He didn't smile or

laugh, but I was the happiest boy in that city.

6 We left New Orleans at four o'clock one afternoon. Mr. Bixby was at the wheel. Here at the beginning of the river, there were a lot of steamboats. Most of them were at landings on the sides of the river. We went past them quickly, very close to them. Suddenly Mr. Bixby said, "Here. You steer her." And he gave me the wheel. My heart was in my mouth. I thought it was very dangerous, close to those other boats. I began to steer into the middle of the river. In the middle, there was enough water for everybody.

7 "What are you doing?" Mr. Bixby cried angrily. He pushed me away and took the wheel again. And again he steered us near the other boats. After a while, he became a little cooler. He told me that water runs fast in the middle of a river. At the sides, it runs slow. "So if you're going up-river, you have to steer near the sides. You can go in the middle only if you're going down-river." Well, that was good enough for me. I decided to be a down-river pilot only.

8 Sometimes Mr. Bixby showed me points of land. "This is Six-Mile Point," he said. The land pointed like a finger into the water. Another time, he said, "This is Nine-Mile Point." It looked like Six-Mile Point to me. Later, he said, "This is Twelve-Mile Point." Well, this wasn't very interesting news. All the points seemed the same.

9 After six hours of this, we had supper and went to bed. Even bed was more interesting than the "points." At midnight, someone put a light in my eyes. "Hey, let's go!"

10 Then he left. I couldn't understand this. I decided to go back to sleep. Soon the man came again with his light; now he was angry. "Wake up!" he called. I was angry, too, and said, "Don't put that light in my eyes! How can I sleep if you wake me up every minute?"

11 All the men in the room laughed at this. The man left again, but came back soon with Mr. Bixby. One minute later I was climbing the steps to the pilot-house. Some of my clothes were on me. The rest were in my hands. Mr. Bixby walked behind me, angry. Now, here was something interesting: Pilots worked in the middle of the night!

12 And that night was a bad one. There was a lot of

mist on the river. You could not see through it. Where were we going? I was frightened. But Mr. Bixby turned the wheel easily and happily. He told me we had to find a farm. Jones Farm. To myself I said, "Okay, Mr. Bixby. You can try all night. But you'll never find anything in this mist."

13 Suddenly Mr. Bixby turned to me and said, "What's the name of the first point above New Orleans?"

14 I answered very quickly. I said I didn't know.

15 "Don't *know?*"

16 The loudness of his voice surprised me. But I couldn't answer him.

17 "Well, then," he said, "What's the name of the next point?"

18 Again I didn't know.

19 "Now, look! After Twelve-Mile Point, where do you cross the river?"

20 "I-I-I don't know."

21 "You-you-you don't know? Well, what *do* you know?"

22 "I—nothing, it seems."

23 "Nothing? *Less* than nothing! You say you want to pilot a steamboat on the river? My boy, you couldn't pilot a cow down a street! Why do you think I told you the names of those points?"

24 "Well, to-to—be interesting, I thought."

25 "What?! To be *interesting?*" Now he was *very* angry. He walked across the pilot-house and back again. This cooled him down. "My boy," he said more softly, "You must get a little notebook. I will tell you many names of places on this river. You must write them all down. Then you must remember them. All of them. That is the only way to become a pilot."

26 My heart fell. I never remembered things easily in school. But also I didn't fully believe Mr. Bixby. No one, I thought, could know all of the Mississippi. No one could put that great river inside his head.

27 Then Mr. Bixby pulled a bell. A worker's voice came up from below.

28 "What's this, sir?"

29 "Jones Farm," Mr. Bixby said.

30 I could see nothing through the mist. And Mr. Bixby could see nothing. I knew that. So I didn't believe him. How could I? We were in the middle of nowhere! But soon the boat's nose softly hit the landing. Workers' voices came up to us. I still couldn't believe it, but this was Jones Farm!

II

31 And so, slowly, I began to put the Mississippi River inside my head. I filled a notebook—I filled two notebooks—with names from the river. Islands, towns, points, bends in the river. The names of all these things went into my notebooks. And slowly some of them began to go into my head. Then more of them. I began to feel better about myself. I was beginning to learn the river.

32 Then one day Mr. Bixby said to me, "What is the shape of Apple Bend?"

33 "The shape of Apple Bend?"

34 "Yes, of course."

35 "I know the *name* of Apple Bend. I know where it is. Don't tell me I have to know the shape of it, too!"

36 Mr. Bixby's mouth went off like a gun, bang! He shot all his bad words at me. Then, as always, he cooled. "My boy," he said, "You must learn the shape of this river and everything on it. If you don't know the shape, you can't steer at night. And of course the river has two shapes. One during the day, and one at night."

37 "Oh, no!"

38 "Oh, yes. Look: How can you walk through a room at home in the dark? Because you know the shape of it. You can't *see* it."

39 "You mean I must know this river like the rooms at home?"

40 "No. I mean you must know it *better* than the rooms at home."

41 "I want to die."

42 "My boy, I don't want you to be sad or angry. But there is more."

43 "All right. Tell me everything. Give it to me!"

44 "I'm sorry, but you must learn these things. There is

no other way. Now, a night with stars throws shadows. Dark shadows change the shape of the river. You think you are coming to a bend, but there *is* no bend. And this is different from a night with no stars. On a night with no stars, the river has a different shape. You think there are no bends, but there *are* bends. And of course, on a night with mist, the river has no shape. You think you are going to steer the boat onto the land. But then suddenly you see that it's water, not land. Well. Then you have your moonlight nights. Different kinds of moonlight change the shape of the river again. And there are different kinds of shadows, too. Different shadows bring different shapes to the river. You see—"

45 "Oh, stop!" I cried. "You mean I have to learn the thousand million different shapes of this river?"

46 "No, no! You only learn *the* shape of the river. The *one* shape. And you steer by that. Don't you understand? You steer by the river that's in your head. Forget the one that's before your eyes."

47 "I see. And you think that's easy."

48 "I never said it was easy. And of course the river is always, always changing shape. The river of this week is different from the river of last week. And next week it will be different again."

49 "All right. Goodbye. I'm going home."

50 But of course I didn't go home. I stayed. I wanted to learn. I *needed* to learn. And day by day, month by month, I did learn. The river was my school. Slowly I began to think I was a good student. I could steer the boat alone, without Mr. Bixby's help. I knew the river like the rooms of my house—no, better. I could steer at night, by the shape of the river in my head. No cub-pilot was better, I thought. Oh, my nose was very high in the air!

51 Of course, Mr. Bixby saw this. And he decided to teach me another lesson.

52 One beautiful summer's day we were near the bend above Island 66. I had the wheel. We were in the middle of the river. It was easy water, deep and wide.

53 Mr. Bixby said, "I am going below for a while. Do

you know how to run the next bend?"

54 A strange question! It was perhaps the easiest bend in the river. I knew it well. It began at a little island. The river was wide there, and more than a hundred feet deep. There was no possible danger.

55 "Know how to *run* it? Why, I can run it with my eyes closed!"

56 "How much water is there in it?"

57 "What kind of question is that? There's more water there than in the Atlantic Ocean."

58 "You think so, do you?"

59 He left, and soon I began to worry. There was something in his voice. . . .

60 I didn't know it, but Mr. Bixby had stayed close to the pilot-house. I couldn't see him, but he was talking to some of the men. Soon a worker came and stood in front of the pilot-house. He looked a little worried. We were near the island at the beginning of the bend. Another man came and stood with the first. He looked worried, too. Then another. They looked at me, then at the water, then at me again. Soon there were fifteen or twenty people out there in front of me. No one said anything. The noise of the engines suddenly seemed loud to me.

61 Then one of them said in a strange voice, "Where is Mr. Bixby?"

62 "Below," I said. The man turned away and said nothing more.

63 Now I became *very* worried. I steered a little to the right. I thought I saw danger! I steered to the left. More danger! I wanted to go slower. I wanted to stop the engines. I didn't know *what* I wanted.

64 In the end I called down to the engine room. "How deep is it here? Can you tell me soon? Please be quick!"

65 "Forty feet," came the voice. He had the answer already! Forty feet! It couldn't be! Why, the water there was as deep as. . . .

66 "Thirty-five," he said in a worried voice. "Thirty-two! Twenty-eight!"

67 I couldn't believe it! I ran to the wheel, pulled a

bell, stopped the engines.

68 "Eighteen!" came the voice. "Fifteen! Thirteen! Ten!"

69 Ten feet! I was filled with fear now. I did not know what to do. I called loudly down to the man in the engine room. "Back!" I called. "Please, Ben, back her! Back her! Oh, Ben, if you love me, back her now!"

70 I heard the door close softly. I looked around, and there stood Mr. Bixby. He smiled a sweet smile at me. Then all the people in front of the pilot-house began to laugh. I understood it all now, and I felt two feet tall. I started the engines again. I steered to the middle of the river without another word. After a while, I said, "That was kind and loving of you, *wasn't* it? I think I'll hear that story the rest of my life."

71 "Well, perhaps you will. And that won't be a bad thing. I want you to learn something from this. Didn't you know there was a hundred feet of water at that bend?"

72 "Yes, I did."

73 "All right, then. If you know a thing, you must believe it—and deeply. The river is in your head, remember? And another thing. If you get into a dangerous place, don't turn and run. That doesn't help. You must fight fear, always. And on the river there is always fear."

74 It was a good lesson, perhaps his best lesson. And I never forgot it. But I can tell you, it cost a lot to learn it. Every day for weeks and weeks I had to hear those difficult words: "Oh, Ben, if you love me, back her!"

A CUB-PILOT'S EDUCATION
EXERCISES

A. Understanding the Main Ideas

Answer the following questions with complete sentences.

1. Why did all the boys in Twain's village want to be steamboat pilots?

2. What did the village look like before the steamboat came every day?

3. Why did Mr. Bixby give the boy the wheel on their first trip up the river? Why did he take it back again?

4. Why was the boy surprised when the boat reached Jones Farm?

5. Did the boy learn slowly or quickly? Why?

6. What was the "best lesson" the boy learned from Mr. Bixby? How did Mr. Bixby teach this lesson?

B. Close Reading

Read the sentence from the story. Then answer the question about the sentence.

Note: Questions 1-6 are about Part I (pages 56-61). Questions 7-12 are about Part II (pages 61-65).

1. "Then a worker cries 'S-t-e-a-m-boat coming!' And everything changes!" (paragraph 3)
What were some of these changes?

2. "So in the end I won." (paragraph 5)
What did the boy win? How did he win it?

3. "I began to steer into the middle of the river." (paragraph 6)
Why did the boy do this?

4. "Well, that was good enough for me. I decided to be a down-river pilot only." (paragraph 7)
Why did the boy decide this? Why was it easier to steer

down-river than up-river?

5. "All the men in the room laughed at this."
(paragraph 11)
What did the men laugh at?

6. "My heart fell." (paragraph 26)
What does this mean? Why did it happen?

7. "And so, slowly, I began to put the Mississippi River inside my head." (paragraph 31)
What made the boy decide to do this? How did he do it?

8. "You steer by the river that's in your head. Forget the one that's before your eyes." (paragraph 46)
Did Mr. Bixby say this about daytime steering or nighttime steering? Why?

9. "Oh, my nose was very high in the air!"
(paragraph 50)
Why did the boy feel so good about himself?

10. "Eighteen!" came the voice. "Fifteen! Thirteen! Ten!"
(paragraph 68)
Why did these numbers frighten the boy? Why did they surprise him?

11. "I understood it all now, and I felt two feet tall."
(paragraph 70)
What did the boy understand? Why did he feel so small?

C. Discussion

1. A Chinese thinker named Confucius said, "I hear, I forget. I see, I remember. I do, I understand." Does Ben learn most by hearing, seeing, or doing? Do you learn best by hearing, seeing, or doing? How do most schools try to teach students?

2. Do you think Mr. Bixby was a good teacher or a bad teacher? Why? Describe the best teacher you had when you were young. What made her or him a good teacher?

D. Vocabulary Practice

Match each word in Column A with the phrase in Column B that has a similar meaning. Write the number of the word next to the correct phrase.

A	B
1. pilot	_____machine
2. steer	_____troubled in the mind
3. shape	_____not safe
4. worried	_____outline; form; appearance
5. engine	_____give direction to
6. dangerous	_____"driver" of a boat or plane

E. Word Forms

From the chart below, choose the form of the word that best fits the sentence that follows it.

Example:

(kind) They showed me a lot of <u>kindness</u> at their home.

Noun	Adjective	Adverb	Verb
kindness	kind	kindly	
peace	peaceful	peacefully	
point	pointed	pointedly	point
worry	worried	worriedly	worry

coolness	cool	coolly	cool
danger	dangerous	dangerously	
loudness	loud	loudly	
easiness	easy	easily	ease
interest	interesting	interestingly	interest

1. (peace) The man who has drunk too much lies _____ near the river.

2. (point) In some places, the land _____ like a finger into the river.

3. (worry) The men in front of the pilot-house haD _____ faces.

4. (cool) He was very angry at first, but after a while, he _____.

5. (danger) The river can be very _____ when it is covered with mist.

6. (loud) The _____ of his voice surprised the boy.

7. (easy) It was the _____ bend in the river.

8. (interest) I didn't tell you those things just to be _____.

F. Language Activity: Crossword Puzzle

On the following page, find the word that explains or completes the sentence, or answers the question. Write the word in the right boxes, one letter for each box. Some words go across, some down. The first letter of each word is given.

Number 1 Across has been done for you.

Across

1. One way to travel down the Mississippi River(S)

2. If you don't know the _____ of the river, you can't find your way at night. (S)

3. Mr. Bixby (P)

4. The boy turned it to the left and to the right. (W)

5. "Why do you think I told you the names of all those points? To be _____?" (I)

Down

1. It can change the shape of the river. (S)

2. Mr. Bixby would usually get _____ before he got cool. (H)

3. What did the boy begin to do with the boat on his first day as cub-pilot? (S)

4. What was the boy in, when Mr. Bixby got him at midnight? (B)

5. The nose of the boat softly touched the _____ at Jones Farm. (L)

6. No one could see through the _____ on the river. (M)

G. Writing: Mr. Bixby and Ben Make Plans

In the story, Ben is the man in the engine room. When the boy calls down to him to ask how deep the water is, he answers "forty feet" — but really the water is much deeper than that. Mr. Bixby has made a plan with Ben to fool the boy.

Write a dialogue between Ben and Mr. Bixby. In your dialogue, show how they made their plan. What do they say, exactly, when they decide that

- they will teach the young cub a lesson
- they will make him think that the deep water is not deep
- they will leave him alone in the pilot house
- they will tell the other workers to come and stand in front of the pilot-house and look worried
- the boy will get worried
- one of the workers will ask for Mr. Bixby. The boy will get even more worried
- he will try to steer away from danger
- he will call down to the engine room to find how deep the water is
- Ben will say "forty feet" at first — then less and less
- the boy will try to stop the boat
- then he . . .
- then . . .

THE LADY, OR THE TIGER?

Before You Read the Story . . .

1. *A Life*

Read the paragraph about Frank Stockton on page 73. In what magazine was this story first published? Who read this magazine? Why do you think the story caused so much excitement?

2. *The Pictures*

Look at the picture on page 75. From their clothes, who are they? When did they live?

The title of the story asks a question. Think about what question it is asking. Now look at the picture on page 79. What does the picture show? Where is the man going? Why is he looking back?

3. *Thinking About It*

A phrase you will read early in the story is: "the first law of Chance." This phrase suggests that chance – or luck – follows certain laws, or rules. Do you agree? Which is more important to you in your life: laws and rules, or chance and luck? Why do you think so?

4. *Skimming*

Look over the following questions. Then skim the story. Read only the first sentence or two of each paragraph. Next, return to the questions below and write an answer to each one. Do not reread. Write only from memory. Skim the story and write answers to the questions in no more than 10 minutes. Compare your answers to those of another student.

Does the story take place in our times, or long ago?

Are the people in the story rich, or poor?

Does the story ask a question, or give an answer?

Is the story like a newspaper article, or a folk tale?

Is the story about peace, or the opposite of peace?

Do you think you will enjoy reading the story? Why or why not?

What are a few interesting words or phrases that you remember reading?

THE LADY, OR THE TIGER?

adapted from the story by
FRANK STOCKTON

Frank R. Stockton was born in 1834. His most famous stories are in the form of fairy tales, ghost stories, or romances. But in all of them his humor has an edge like a knife. When "The Lady, or the Tiger?" was published in *Century Magazine* in 1882, it caused excitement all over the country. Hundreds of people wrote letters to the magazine or to their newspapers about it. Many letters demanded an answer to the question that the story asks. Others asked if the story was really about government, or psychology, or the battle of the sexes, or something else. Wisely, Stockton never answered any of the letters. The story remains as fresh today as it was then. Frank Stockton died in 1902.

A long, long time ago, there was a semi-barbaric king. I call him semi-barbaric because the modern world, with its modern ideas, had softened his barbarism a little. But still, his ideas were large, wild, and free. He had a wonderful imagination. Since he was also a king of the greatest powers, he easily turned the dreams of his imagination into facts. He greatly enjoyed talking to himself about ideas. And, when he and himself agreed upon a thing, the thing was done. He was a very pleasant man when everything in his world moved smoothly. And when something went wrong, he became even more pleasant. Nothing, you see, pleased him more than making wrong things right.

2 One of this semi-barbaric king's modern ideas was the idea of a large arena. In this arena, his people could watch both men and animals in acts of bravery.

3 But even this modern idea was touched by the king's wild imagination. In his arena, the people saw more than soldiers fighting soldiers, or men fighting animals. They enjoyed more than the sight of blood. In the king's arena, the people saw the laws of the country at work. They saw good men lifted up and bad men pushed down. Most important, they were able to watch the workings of the first law of Chance.

4 Here is what happened when a man was accused of a crime. If the king was interested in the crime, then the people were told to come to the arena. They came together and sat there, thousands of them. The king sat high up in his king's chair. When he gave a sign, a door below him opened. The accused man stepped out into the arena. Across from him, on the other side of the arena, were two other doors. They were close together and they looked the same. The accused man would walk straight to these doors and open one of them. He could choose either one of the

doors. He was forced by nothing and led by no one. Only Chance helped him—or didn't help him.

5 Behind one of the doors was a tiger. It was the wildest, biggest, hungriest tiger that could be found. Of course, it quickly jumped on the man. The man quickly—or not so quickly—died. After he died, sad bells rang, women cried, and the thousands of people walked home slowly.

6 But, if the accused man opened the other door, a lady would step out. She was the finest and most beautiful lady that could be found. At that moment, there in the arena, she would be married to the man. It didn't matter if the man was already married. It didn't matter if he was in love with another woman. The king did not let little things like that get in the way of his imagination. No, the two were married there in front of the king. There was music and dancing. Then happy bells rang, women cried, and the thousands of people walked home singing.

7 This was the way the law worked in the king's semi-barbaric country. Its fairness is clear. The criminal could not know which door the lady was behind. He opened either door as he wanted. At the moment he opened the door, he did not know if he was going to be eaten or married.

8 The people of the country thought the law was a good one. They went to the arena with great interest. They never knew if they would see a bloody killing or a lovely marriage. This uncertainty gave the day its fine and unusual taste. And they liked the fairness of the law. Wasn't it true that the accused man held his life in his own hands?

9 This semi-barbaric king had a daughter. The princess was as beautiful as any flower in the king's imagination. She had a mind as wild and free as the king's. She had a heart like a volcano. The king loved her deeply, watched her closely, and was very jealous of her. But he could not always watch her. And in his castle lived a young man. This young man was a worker. He was a good worker, but he was of low birth. He was brave and handsome, and the princess loved him, and was jealous of him. Because of

the girl's semi-barbarism, her love was hot and strong.
Of course, the young man quickly returned it. The lovers were happy together for many months. But one day the king discovered their love. Of course he did not lose a minute. He threw the young man into prison and named a day for his appearance in the arena.

10 There had never been a day as important as that one. The country was searched for the strongest, biggest, most dangerous tiger. With equal care, the country was searched for the finest and most beautiful young woman. There was no question, of course, that the young man had loved the princess. He knew it, she knew it, the king knew it, and everybody else knew it, too. But the king didn't let this stand in the way of his excellent law. Also, the king knew that the young man would now disappear from his daughter's life. He would disappear with the other beautiful lady. Or he would disappear into the hungry tiger. The only question was, "Which?"

11 And so the day arrived. Thousands and thousands of people came to the arena. The king was in his place, across from those two doors that seemed alike but were truly very different.

12 All was ready. The sign was given. The door below the king opened, and the lover of the princess walked into the arena. Tall, handsome, fair, he seemed like a prince. The people had not known that such a fine young man had lived among them. Was it any wonder that the princess had loved him?

13 The young man came forward into the arena, and then turned toward the king's chair. But his eyes were not on the king. They were on the princess, who sat to her father's right. Perhaps it was wrong for the young lady to be there. But remember that she was still semi-barbaric. Her wild heart would not let her be away from her lover on this day. More important, she now knew the secret of the doors. Over the past few days, she had used all of her power in the castle, and much of her gold. She had discovered which door hid the tiger, and which door hid the lady.

14 She knew more than this. She knew the lady. It was

one of the fairest and loveliest ladies in the castle. In fact, this lady was more than fair and lovely. She was thoughtful, kind, loving, full of laughter, and quick of mind. The princess hated her. She had seen, or imagined she had seen, the lady looking at the young man. She thought these looks had been noticed and even returned. Once or twice she had seen them talking together. Perhaps they had talked for only a moment. Perhaps they had talked of nothing important. But how could the princess be sure of that? The other girl was lovely and kind, yes. But she had lifted her eyes to the lover of the princess. And so, in her semi-barbaric heart, the princess was jealous, and hated her.

15 Now, in the arena, her lover turned and looked at her. His eyes met hers, and he saw at once that she knew the secret of the doors. He had been sure that she would know it. He understood her heart. He had known that she would try to learn this thing which no one else knew—not even the king. He had known she would try. And now, as he looked at her, he saw that she had succeeded.

16 At that moment, his quick and worried look asked the question: "Which?" This question in his eyes was as clear to the princess as spoken words. There was no time to lose. The question had been asked in a second. It must be answered in a second.

17 Her right arm rested on the arm of her chair. She lifted her hand and made a quick movement towards the right. No one saw except her lover. Every eye except his was on the man in the arena.

18 He turned and walked quickly across the empty space. Every heart stopped beating. Every breath was held. Every eye was fixed upon that man. Without stopping for even a second, he went to the door on the right and opened it.

19 Now, the question is this: Did the tiger come out of that door, or did the lady?

20 As we think deeply about this question, it becomes harder and harder to answer. We must know the heart of the animal called man. And the heart is difficult to know.

Think of it, dear reader, and remember that the decision is not yours. The decision belongs to that hot-blooded, semi-barbaric princess. Her heart was at a white heat beneath the fires of jealousy and painful sadness. She had lost him, but who should have him?

21 Very often, in her thoughts and in her dreams, she had cried out in fear. She had imagined her lover as he opened the door to the hungry tiger.

22 And even more often she had seen him at the other door! She had bitten her tongue and pulled her hair. She had hated his happiness when he opened the door to the lady. Her heart burned with pain and hatred when she imagined the scene: He goes quickly to meet the woman. He leads her into the arena. His eyes shine with new life. The happy bells ring wildly. The two of them are married before her eyes. Children run around them and throw flowers. There is music, and the thousands of people dance in the streets. And the princess's cry of sadness is lost in the

sounds of happiness!

23 Wouldn't it be better for him to die at once? Couldn't he wait for her in the beautiful land of the semi-barbaric future?

24 But the tiger, those cries of pain, that blood!

25 Her decision had been shown in a second. But it had been made after days and nights of deep and painful thought. She had known she would be asked. She had decided what to answer. She had moved her hand to the right.

26 The question of her decision is not an easy one to think about. Certainly I am not the one person who should have to answer it. So I leave it with all of you: Which came out of the opened door—the lady, or the tiger?

THE LADY, OR THE TIGER?
EXERCISES

A. Understanding the Main Ideas

If the sentence below is true, write "T" next to it. If it is not true, write "F" for false, then rewrite the sentence so that it is true.

_____ **1.** The king and the princess were civilized people.

_____ **2.** The king believed that questions of right and wrong should be decided by chance.

_____ **3.** There were three doors in the arena. Behind one stood the king, behind the second stood the princess, and behind the third stood the tiger.

_____ **4.** The people of the land thought the king was fair.

_____ **5.** The king was pleased that the princess and the young man were in love. He wanted them to be married in the arena.

_____ **6.** The princess was very upset because she couldn't help her lover choose the right door.

____ **7.** The young man didn't know which door to choose.

B. Close Reading: Understanding Pronouns

In the following sentences, the words <u>this</u>, <u>that</u>, and <u>it</u> have been underlined. Find the sentence in the story (paragraph numbers are given). Then tell what words or ideas are meant by <u>this</u>, <u>that</u>, or <u>it</u>.

Examples:

"The young man quickly returned <u>it</u>." (paragraph 9)

"<u>It</u> means: the princess's love.

"She knew more than <u>this</u>." (paragraph 14)

"<u>This</u>" means: which door hid the tiger, and which door hid the lady.

1. The king did not let little things like <u>that</u> get in the way of his imagination. (paragraph 6)
2. <u>This</u> was the way the law worked in the king's semi-barbaric country. (paragraph 7)
3. <u>This</u> uncertainty gave the day its fine and unusual taste. (What uncertainty?) (paragraph 8)
4. But the king didn't let <u>this</u> stand in the way of his excellent law. (paragraph 10)
5. But how could the princess be sure of <u>that</u>? (paragraph 14)
6. He had been sure that she would know <u>it</u>. (paragraph 15)
7. Certainly I am not the one person who should have to answer <u>it</u>. (paragraph 26)

C. Discussion

1. "Which came out of the opened door — the lady, or the tiger?" What do you think? Did the princess send her lover to the lady or to the tiger? Why?

2. The end of "The Lady, or the Tiger?" is about the princess's decision: that is, whether to send her lover to the lady or to the tiger. But doesn't the lover, too, have a decision to make? Look at the picture on page 75. The lover is about to open one of the doors. In this picture, he turns and takes a final look at the princess. With a movement of her hand, she has told him to open the door on the right. This leads us to a final question. Remember, the lover knows that the princess knows which door hides the lady, and which door hides the tiger. How well does the lover know the princess? Will he open the door she has chosen? Or, believing it hides the tiger, will he open the other one? Why, finally, did he open the door on the right?

3. Do you think people are less barbaric now than they were hundreds of years ago? In what ways? Are they more barbaric? In what ways? Or are they exactly the same? Give specific examples to help others understand your thoughts.

D. Vocabulary Practice

Choose the best word from the list below, and fill in the blanks in the sentences.

volcano	imagination
accused	jealous
arena	chance
fair	semi-barbaric

1. The _____ laws of that land were made by the king.

2. People gathered in the _____ to see what

would happen to the young man.

3. Only _____ helped a man decide which door to choose.

4. If someone broke a law, he was _____ of the crime. Then he had to come before the king in the arena.

5. The king had some modern ideas. But his ideas were touched by his wild _____.

6. The love in the princess' heart was a strong as a hot

_____.

7. The princess felt _____ of the beautiful, gentle lady in the castle.

8. Everyone thought the working of chance was _____ because a man's life was in his own hands.

E. Word Forms: Verb, Noun, Adjective

Put the correct form of the word on the left into the blank spaces in the sentences.

1. (marry / marriage / married) Although the princess loved the young man, the king was against their _____. If an accused man chose the door with the lady behind it, he had to _____. It didn't matter if he was already _____.

2. (accuse / accusation / accused) It was a matter of chance whether the _____ chose the lady or the tiger. The king _____ the young man of loving his daughter. Neither the princess nor the young man denied the _____.

3. (imagine / imagination / imaginative) The king was an _____ man. His laws reflected his wild _____. Can you _____ how people would feel about such a law today?

4. (search / search / searching) The young man gave the princess a _____ look. He was sure she must know which door hid the tiger. The princess _____ her heart to decide which door to show him. No matter which door he chose, she would have to continue her own _____ for a husband.

5. (disappear / disappearance) The accused would _____ into the tiger's mouth, or into the lady's arms. Which _____ do you think was worse for the princess?

6. (Succeed / success / successful) The princess _____ in giving her lover a sign. But the reader doesn't know whether the young man makes a _____ choice. And we don't know which choice would seem like a _____ to the princess.

F. Language Practice: Pair Work on Composition

With a partner, read over the instructions for the Writing exercise (Exercise G) below. Share the ideas you both have about each of the three paragraphs. Take notes as you talk. Plan each paragraph separately. Next, working alone, write the three paragraphs. Then, exchange your paragraphs with the paragraphs of your partner. Correct your partner's paragraphs. Make suggestions for the improvement of the paragraphs your partner wrote. Discuss the suggestions your partner makes on your paragraphs. Then rewrite them.

G. Writing: Three-paragraph Composition

"Which came out of the opened door, the lady or the tiger?"

Write down the above question. Then write a paragraph that begins with the sentence, "Perhaps it was the lady who came out." Give at least three reasons why the princess chose the lady for her lover.

Then write a second paragraph that begin, "On the other hand, perhaps it was the tiger." Give at least three reasons why the princess chose the tiger.

Then write a third paragraph that begins with the words, "Personally, I think . . ." Give your own choice. Which of the reasons that you have written is the most important to you? Why?

AN OCCURRENCE AT OWL CREEK BRIDGE

Before You Read the Story . . .

1. *A Life*

Read the paragraph about Ambrose Bierce on page 87. How many years did Bierce go to school? Which other writers in this book had little or no school education?

2. *The Pictures*

Look at the pictures on pages 89 and 92. On page 89, we see a man with a rope around his neck. How would you describe his clothes? What sort of a man does he seem to be, judging by these clothes? On page 92, we see where the man is standing. How would you describe the clothes of the other man in the picture? What does his profession seem to be, judging by these clothes?

What is the name of the bridge in the picture on page 92? (Hint: the title tells you.) What is a synonym for the word "occurrence" in the title?

3. *Thinking About It . . .*

The paragraph about Ambrose Bierce on page 87 mentions "the Civil War between the North and the South." This war took place in the United States between 1861-1865. In a civil war, people of the same community fight against each other. What do you think are the worst effects of a civil war?

4. *Scanning*

You are asked to find Ambrose Bierce's age, in years, at some of the major events in his interesting life. To the left of each statement below, write Bierce's age at the time the event took place. To do this, you will have to scan the paragraph about Bierce on page 87 and make calculations based on the information you find. Try to complete the entire exercise in three minutes or less.

_____ Bierce joins the army.

_____ His first short story is published.

_____ He goes with his wife to London.

_____ He returns to the United States.

_____ He disappears in the Mexican War.

_____ "An Occurrence at Owl Creek Bridge" is

published in a collection of stories.

AN OCCURRENCE AT OWL CREEK BRIDGE

adapted from the story by
AMBROSE BIERCE

Ambrose Bierce was born in Ohio in 1842. He went to school, a military academy, for just one year. In 1864, during the Civil War between the North and the South, Bierce joined the Army. After the war he went to California. He wrote political pieces for newspapers. His first short story was published in 1871. That same year he married and went to live in London. After five years in London he returned to the United States. He worked for the Hearst Newspaper Company on the West Coast. He went to write about the Mexican War in 1914, where he disappeared in the fighting. "An Occurrence at Owl Creek Bridge" appeared in a collection of short stories, *Tales of Soldiers and Civilians*, in 1891. A second collection, *Can Such Things Be?*, was published in 1893.

I

A man stood upon a railroad bridge in northern Alabama. He looked down into the river below. The man's hands were tied behind his back. A rope circled his neck. The end of the long rope was tied to part of the wooden bridge above his head.

2 Next to the man stood two soldiers of the Northern army. A short distance away stood their captain. Two soldiers guarded each end of the bridge. On one bank of the river, other soldiers stood silently, facing the bridge. The two guards at each end of the bridge faced the banks of the river. None of the soldiers moved. The captain, too, stood silent. He watched the work of the two soldiers near him, but he made no sign. All of them were waiting silently for Death. Death is a visitor who must be met with respect. Even soldiers, who see so much death, must show respect to Death. And in the army, silence and stillness are signs of respect.

3 The man with the rope around his neck was going to be hanged. He was about thirty-five years old. He was not dressed like a soldier. He wore a well-fitting coat. His face was a fine one. He had a straight nose, strong mouth, and dark hair. His large eyes were gray, and looked kind. He did not seem like the sort of man to be hanged. Clearly he was not the usual sort of criminal. But the Army has laws for hanging many kinds of people. And gentlemen are not excused from hanging.

4 When the two soldiers were ready, they stepped away. The captain faced the condemned man. They stood face to face on a piece of wood. The middle of the board rested against the edge of the bridge. When the captain stepped off the board, the piece of wood would fall down into the river. The condemned man would fall down after the board. Only the rope around his neck would stop him. He

would be hanged by the neck until dead. The man's face had not been covered. His eyes were open. He looked down at the river below. He saw a small piece of wood floating along with the river. How slowly it moved! What a gentle river!

5 He closed his eyes and thought of his wife and children. Until now, other things had filled his mind: the water, painted gold by the sun . . . the soldiers . . . the floating wood. After a little while he heard a new sound. A strange metallic sound kept beating through the thoughts of his family. He wondered what it was. It sounded far away, and yet very close. It was as slow as a death-bell ringing. The sound came louder and louder. It seemed to cut into his brain like a knife. He was afraid he would cry out. But it was only his own watch making its little sound.

6 He opened his eyes. He saw again the water below him. "If I could free my hands," he thought, "I might throw off the rope. I could jump into the river. If I swam quickly underwater, I could escape the bullets. I would reach the river bank, run into the woods and go home. My home, thank God, is still safe from the Northern Army." These thoughts must be written in words here. But they passed as quickly as light through the condemned man's mind.

7 And then the captain stepped off the board.

II

8 The condemned man's name was Peyton Farquhar. He was a rich farmer, the last son in an old Alabama family. He owned slaves who worked on his farm. Like other Southern farmers, he believed that slaves were necessary to Southern farming. The Northern government had said that it was against the law to have slaves. Now, the North and the South were at war.

9 Certain work had kept Peyton Farquhar from joining the Southern Army at the beginning of the war. But he was at heart a soldier. He did everything he could to help the South. No job was too low, no adventure too dangerous. One evening, Farquhar and his wife were sitting in the garden. A soldier rode up to the house. He was dressed like

other soldiers in the Southern Army. While Mrs. Farquhar went to get him a drink of water, the soldier spoke with Farquhar.

10 "The Northerners are rebuilding the railroads," the soldier said. "They are getting ready for another advance. They've reached Owl Creek Bridge. They've fixed the bridge and moved in a lot of soldiers. Anyone who attacks the railroad or tries to destroy the bridge will be hanged."

11 "How far is it to Owl Creek Bridge?" Farquhar asked.

12 "About thirty miles."

13 "Are there soldiers on this side of the bridge?"

14 "Only a few guards."

15 "Suppose that a man went around the guards?" Farquhar smiled. "What could he do to stop the advance?"

16 The soldier thought a moment. Then he said, "I was at the bridge a month ago. I saw a lot of wood that the river had washed against one end of the bridge. It's very dry now, and the wood would burn quickly and well."

17 The lady had now brought the water. The soldier drank. He thanked her, bowed to Farquhar, and rode away. An hour later, after nightfall, he passed Farquhar's farm again. He went North in the direction he had come from. He was a Northern soldier.

III

18 Peyton Farquhar fell down from the bridge. He lost consciousness. He was like one already dead. He was awakened—hours later, it seemed to him—by the great pain in his neck. Pain passed through his body like rivers of fire. He was conscious of a fullness in his head. He could not think. He could only feel. He was conscious of motion. He seemed to be falling through a red cloud. Then suddenly the light flew upward with the noise of a loud splash. A fearful noise was in his ears. All was cold and dark. The power of thought came back to him. He knew the rope had broken, and he had fallen into the river. The rope around his neck was cutting off the air. To die of hanging at the bottom of a river! No! Impossible! He opened his eyes

in the darkness. He saw light far, far above him. He was still going down, for the light grew smaller and smaller. But then it grew brighter, and he knew he was coming back up to the top of the river. Now he felt sorry to be coming out of the water. He had been so comfortable. "To be hanged and drowned," he thought. "That is not so bad. But I do not want to be shot. No, I will not be shot. That's not fair!"

19 He was not conscious of his actions until he felt pain in his hands. Then he realized that he was trying to free his hands. At last the rope fell off. His arms floated upward; he could see his hands. He watched with interest. His hands were trying to untie the rope around his neck. They pulled off the rope and it floated away. "Put it back, put it back," he felt himself crying. His neck hurt badly. His mind was on fire, his heart beat wildly enough to leave his body. His whole body was in great pain. But his hands pushed him up out of the water. And he took a great breath of air.

20 Now he was fully conscious. His five senses seemed unusually clear. The pain his body had felt made him see and feel the beauty around him. He felt the water against his skin. He heard the soft sound as it hit his neck and shoulders. He looked into the forest on the bank and could see each tree, each leaf. He could even see small forest animals between the trees. A fish swam before his eyes. He noticed how the sunlight shone on the fish's silver skin.

21 He was facing away from the bridge when his head came out of the water. Now he turned around. He saw small men on the bridge, dark against the blue sky. They cried out and pointed at him. The captain took out his gun but did not shoot.

22 Then, suddenly, he heard a loud bang. Something hit the water near his head. Water splashed in his face. He heard a second shot and a light blue cloud rose from the gun. Then Farquhar heard the captain call to the men: "Ready, men . . . Shoot!"

23 Farquhar swam deep under the water. The water sounded loud in his ears. But even above the sound of the water he heard the shots. He swam down the river.

24 Later he swam to the top again. He saw he was quite far from the bridge. The soldiers were still pointing their guns at him.

25 "The captain will not order them to shoot together again," he thought. "It's as easy to escape many bullets as one. He'll order them to shoot as they wish. God help me, I cannot escape them all."

26 Suddenly he was caught by a strong current in the river. The current pulled him under the water. It carried him down the river and turned him over and over. At last the force of the current pushed him up onto the bank.

27 He lay on the bank, crying with happiness and tiredness. He dug his fingers into the river bank. The small stones felt like jewels. The trees looked to him like a forest of gold. The air smelled clean and sweet, and a pink light shone through the trees.

28 The sound of bullets in the trees awoke him. He rose to his feet, frightened again, and disappeared into the forest.

29 All that day he traveled. The forest seemed endless. He could find no road. He hadn't realized before now that he lived near such a wild place.

30 When night began to fall, he was very tired and hungry. The thought of his wife and children helped him to continue. At last he found a road that seemed to lead in the right direction. It was as wide and straight as a city street. But it seemed untraveled. There were no fields, no houses nearby. The big black trees formed a straight wall on both sides. Overhead, great golden stars shone in the sky. The stars looked unfamiliar. He was sure that they were grouped in some strange order which meant bad luck. From inside the forest came strange noises. Among them he heard people talking in an unknown language.

31 His neck was in pain. He knew that the rope had left a black circle on his skin. He could not close his eyes. His tongue was dry; he felt very thirsty. Grass seemed to cover the road now; it was soft under his feet.

32 Did he fall asleep while he was walking? Now he sees something else. Perhaps he was wakened from a

dream. Now he stands not far from the door of his own house. Everything looks just as he left it, bright and beautiful in the morning sunshine. He must have traveled through the whole night. As he walks toward the door, his wife appears to meet him. She stands waiting, cool and sweet, silent and still. She holds out her arms to him with a smile of happiness. Ah! how beautiful she is! He moves toward her with open arms. He moves slowly, closer, closer. At the moment he touches her, he feels a great pain at the back of his neck. A while light flames all about him. . . .

33 There was a loud bang, then silence. All was darkness . . .

34 Peyton Farquhar was dead. His body, with a broken neck, hung from a rope beneath Owl Creek Bridge.

AN OCCURRENCE AT OWL CREEK BRIDGE EXERCISES

A. Understanding the Main Ideas

Answer the following questions with complete sentences.

1. At the beginning of the story, where is the man named Farquhar standing?
2. Why were all the soldiers so silent?
3. What would happen when the captain stepped off one end of the board?
4. What sounded so loud to Farquhar? Why?
5. Who was Peyton Farquhar? What role did he play in the war?
6. When Farquhar fell from the bridge, did the rope around his neck break, or did his neck break? What really happened? How do you know?
7. In your opinion, what is the "loud bang" that Farquhar hears (at the very end of the story)?
8. How long do you think it took for Farquhar's escape and adventure to pass through his mind?

B. Close Reading: Adverbial Clauses

To do the exercise below, you will need to read Part II of the story (pages 90-91) carefully. The first half of each sentence below is joined to the second half by an adverb. The adverb tells the relationship of the first half of the sentence to the second half. Make sure that the whole sentence, and not just the separate halves of it, are true.

Finish each sentence below with clause **a, b, c,** or **d.**

1. Peyton Farquhar owned slaves
   a. until he understood that it was against the law.
   b. before he was a rich farmer.
   c. because he thought the South needed slaves.
   d. while the slaves wanted to work for him.

2. A man dressed like a Southern soldier came to Farquhar's house
   a. because he knew that Farquhar had helped the South in the war.
   b. before Farquhar had helped the South in the war.
   c. since he wanted to burn Owl Creek Bridge.
   d. when he learned that the North and South were at war.

3. Farquhar decided to burn the bridge
   a. while the Northerners were rebuilding the railroads.
   b. before the Northerners fixed the bridge and moved in some soldiers.
   c. because Owl Creek Bridge was thirty miles from his home.
   d. after the soldier told him about the dry wood.

4. The soldier rode north
   a. until night came
   b. before Mrs. Farquhar could bring him a drink of water
   c. because he wanted to tell the Northern army about Farquhar.

d. since he wanted to attack the Northern army.

C. Discussion

1. Did the end of the story surprise you? Why, or why not?

2. Find five things that Farquhar thought about before the captain stepped off the board. (see especially paragraphs 4, 5, and 6.) Why do you think that Bierce tells us that these thoughts "passed as quickly as light through the condemned man's mind?" What are the other signs that Farquhar's five senses are working unusually quickly or sharply?

3. In Part III (pages 91-95), what seems very realistic? (Give at least three examples of realistic writing.) What seems unrealistic, dreamlike, or strange? (Give at least three examples of this dreamlike writing.)

D. Vocabulary Practice

The following phrases are definitions of words in the reading. Find the appropriate word, then write it in the blank.

1. To look up to, or admire, something or someone greater than yourself (paragraph 2)

_____

2. A person who breaks the law (paragraph 3)

_____

3. To be allowed *not* to do something (paragraph 3)

_____

4. A person who the law has decided to punish (paragraph 4)

_____

5. To get away from something dangerous (paragraph 6)

_____

6. A move forward (paragraph 10)

_____

7. Of a clear head, clear mind (paragraph 18)

_____

8. Tell someone to do something (paragraph 25)

_____

9. The strong motion of a river or sea (paragraph 26)

_____

10. Vanished, went out of sight (paragraph 28)

_____

11. Empty of traffic or people (paragraph 30)

_____

E. Word Forms: Nouns and Adjectives

Choose the noun or adjective from the left that best fits the sentence to the right.

1. (metal / metallic) Farquhar's watch ticked with a
   _____ sound.

2. (circle / circular) The rope made a _____ path
   around Farquhar's neck.

3. (respect / respectful) The soldiers waited in
   _____ silence for Farquhar's death.

4. (condemnation / condemned) After his _____
   Farquhar was sentenced to death by hanging.

5. (danger / dangerous) Farquhar wanted to help the
   Southern army. He was not afraid of _____.

6. (consciousness / conscious) When he fell from the
   bridge, Farquhar lost _____ as the rope
   tightened around his neck.

7. (traveler / traveled) The road to Farquhar's house was
   not much _____.

8. (order / orderly) The soldiers stood in an
   _____ line, pointing their guns at
   Farquhar.

F. Language Activity: Images for a Silent Movie

Work in pairs or small groups. You will present to the
class 6-10 pictures that tell a part of the story of "An
Occurrence at Owl Creek Bridge." Choose a section of
the story from either Part I (pages 88-90) or Part III
(pages 91-95).

Try to imagine what the camera would see in a silent
movie (a movie without words) of this part of the story.
You do not have to be an artist to draw the pictures. Use
simple lines and "stick figures" to give the idea (see
example, below). If you can, draw the pictures on large
pieces of paper so that they are easy to see.

When you present your pictures to the class, describe what is happening in each one. What does the audience see? What do you want the audience to feel?

G. Writing: A Summary

A summary tells in a few words what someone else said or wrote in many words.

Write a summary of Part I, Part II, or Part III of "An Occurrence at Owl Creek Bridge." Begin your summary with the first sentence of the section you have chosen:

A man stood upon a railroad bridge in Alabama.

or

The condemned man's name was Peyton Farquhar.

or

Peyton Farquhar fell down from the bridge.

In no more than 6 or 8 sentences, tell what happens in the rest of the section you have chosen. Try to include the facts you think are the most important for a general understanding of that section.

A WHITE HERON

Before You Read the Story . . .

1. *A Life*

Read the paragraph about Sarah Orne Jewett on page 103. What subjects does she write about? Where do her stories take place? What other writers in this book write mostly about one particular place?

2. *The Pictures*

Look at the picture on page 105. What can you tell about the place they live in? What is the young man holding?

In the picture on page 108 the girl is at the top of a tall pine tree. What will she be able to do from so high? What kind of bird is flying past her? (Hint: The title tells you.) What do you know about this bird? What can you find out about it?

3. *Thinking About It . . .*

"A White Heron" takes place more than a hundred years ago. The story's main characters live deep in the country, far from cities or towns or even villages. How do you feel about the wild country? Have you spent time there? Would you like to live there? Why, or why not?

4. *Rapid Scanning*

Sometimes we have to quickly scan an entire book, or sections of a book, for specific information. In this exercise, you are asked to scan the biographies of all the writers in GREAT AMERICAN STORIES I. First, read the questions below. Then scan the biographies of the writers to find the answers. Try to do the entire exercise in no more than five minutes.

a. Did these writers write in the 19th century, or in the 20th century?

b. List which ones were men. List which ones were women.

c. How many of them died in the 20th century?

d. How many traveled outside the United States for long periods of time?

e. How many of them were known for their stories about specific places within the United States?

A WHITE HERON

adapted from the story by
SARAH ORNE JEWETT

Sarah Orne Jewett was born in 1849 in South Berwick, Maine. She lived there quietly near the sea most of her life. She wrote stories about the simple lives of the country people around her. Her stories show her love of nature, as well as human nature. The woods, fields, and animals of Maine are almost like characters in her stories. Her best-known book is called *Country of the Pointed Firs*. Maine is well known for its pine and fir trees. In 1909, Sarah Orne Jewett died in the same house in which she had been born and raised.

I

The woods were already filled with shadows one June evening just before eight o'clock. Sylvia was driving her cow home. They turned deep into the dark woods. Their feet knew the way. The birds in the trees above her head seemed to sing "good night" to each other quietly. The air was soft and sweet. Sylvia felt a part of the gray shadows and the moving leaves. To Sylvia, it seemed as if she hadn't really been alive before she came to live with her grandmother in this beautiful place.

2 Suddenly she heard a call. Not a bird's call, which would have had a friendly sound. It was a young man's call, sudden and loud. Sylvia left the cow alone and hid behind some leaves. But the young man saw her.

3 "Halloa, little girl. How far is it to the road?"

4 Sylvia was afraid. She answered in a soft voice, "A good ways . . ."

5 "I'm hunting for some birds," the young man said kindly. He carried a gun over his shoulder. "I am lost and need a friend very much. Don't be afraid. Speak up, and tell me what your name is. Do you think I can spend the night at your house and go out hunting in the morning?"

6 Sylvia was more afraid than ever. But she said her name, and dropped her head like a broken flower.

7 Her grandmother was waiting at the door. The cow gave a "moo" as the three arrived.

8 "Yes, you should speak for yourself, you old cow," said her grandmother. "Where was she hiding so long, Sylvy?"

9 Sylvia didn't speak. She thought her grandmother should be afraid of the stranger.

10 But the young man stood his gun beside the door. He dropped a heavy gun-bag beside it. He said good evening and told the old woman his story.

11 "Dear me, yes," she answered. "You might do better if you went out to the road a mile away. But you're welcome to what we've got. I'll milk the cow right away. Now, you make yourself at home. Sylvy, step round, and set a plate for the gentleman!"

12 Sylvia stepped. She was glad to have something to do, and she was hungry.

13 The young man was surprised to find such a comfortable, clean house in the deep woods of Maine. He thought this was the best supper he had eaten in a month. After supper the new-made friends sat in the shadowed doorway to watch the moon come up. The young man listened happily to the grandmother's stories. The old woman talked most about her children. About her daughter, Sylvia's mother, who had a hard life with so many children. About her son, Dan, who left home for California many years ago.

14 "Sylvy is like Dan," she said happily. "She knows every foot of the woods. She plays with the woods animals and feeds the birds. Yes, she'd give her own meals to them, if I didn't watch her!"

15 "So Sylvy knows all about birds, does she?" asked the young man. "I am trying to catch one of every kind."

16 "Do you keep them alive?" asked the old woman.

17 "No. I stuff them in order to save them," he answered. "I have almost a hundred of them. And I caught every one myself."

18 Sylvia was watching a toad jump in the moonlight.

19 "I followed a bird here that I want to catch. A white heron. You would know a heron if you saw it, Sylvy," he said, hopefully. "A strange, tall white bird with long, thin legs."

20 Sylvia's heart stopped. She knew that strange white bird.

21 "I want that bird more than anything," the young man went on. "I would give ten dollars to know where its nest is."

22 Sylvia couldn't believe there was so much money in the world. But she watched the toad and said nothing.

23 The next day Sylvia went with the young man into the woods. He was kind and friendly, and told her many things about the birds. She wasn't afraid of him anymore. Perhaps in her heart a dream of love was born. But she couldn't understand why he killed and stuffed the birds he liked so much.

II

24 At the edge of the woods a great pine tree stood. Sylvia knew it well. That night she thought of the tree. If she climbed it early in the morning, she could see the whole world. Couldn't she watch the heron fly, and find its hidden nest? What an adventure it would be! And how happy her friend would be! The young man and the old woman slept well that night, but Sylvia thought of her adventure. She forgot to think of sleep. At last, when the night birds stopped singing, she quietly left the house.

25 There was the tall pine tree, still asleep in the moonlight. First she climbed a smaller tree next to it. Then she made the dangerous step across to the old pine. The birds in the woods below her were waking up. She must climb faster if she wanted to see the heron as it left its nest. The tree seemed to grow taller as she went up. The pine tree must have been surprised to feel this small person climbing up. It must have loved this new animal in its arms. Perhaps it moved its branches a little, to help her climb. Sylvia's face shone like a star when she reached the top. She was tired, but very happy. She could see ships out to sea. Woods and farms lay for miles and miles around her. The birds sang louder and louder. At last the sun came up. Where was the heron's nest? Look, look, Sylvia! A white spot rises up from the green trees below. The spot grows larger. The heron flies close. A wild, light bird, wide wings, and a long thin neck. He stops in the tree beyond Sylvia. Wait, wait, Sylvia! Do not move a foot or a finger, to frighten it away!

26 A moment later, Sylvia sighs. A large company of noisy birds comes to the tree, and the heron goes away. It flies down to its home in the green world below. Sylvia

knows its secret now. She climbs back down. Now she is almost crying. Her fingers hurt, and her feet slip. She wonders what the young man will say to her. What will he think when she tells him how to find the heron's nest?

27 "Sylvy, Sylvy," her grandmother called, but nobody answered.

28 The young man woke up and dressed. He wanted to begin hunting again. He was sure Sylvia knew something about the white heron. Here she comes now. Her small face is white, her old dress is torn and dirty. The grandmother and the young man wait at the door to question her. The time has come to tell about the heron's nest.

29 But Sylvia does not speak. The young man looks into her eyes. He will make them rich. She wants to make him happy. He waits to hear the story she can tell.

30 No, she must keep silent! What is it that keeps her quiet? This is the first time the world has put out a hand to her. Does she have to push it away because of a bird? She hears again the wind blowing in the pine tree. She remembers how the white heron flew through the golden air. She remembers how they watched the sea and the morning together. Sylvia cannot speak. She cannot tell the heron's secret and give its life away.

31 Poor Sylvia! She was sad when the young man went away. She could have helped him. She would have followed him like a dog. She would have loved him as a dog loves! Many nights afterwards Sylvia remembered his "Halloa" as she came home with the cow. She forgot the sharp sound of his gun. She forgot the birds, wet with blood. Were the birds better friends than the hunter? Who can tell?

32 Oh, Woods! Oh, Summertime! Remember what riches were lost to her. Bring her your riches instead, your beauties and your gifts. Tell all your secrets to this lonely country child!

A WHITE HERON
EXERCISES

A. Understanding the Main Ideas

Answer the following questions with complete sentences.

1. At the beginning of the story, why was Sylvia afraid of the young man?
2. How does the grandmother act with the young man?
3. Why is the young man killing birds?
4. Why does he say he will pay ten dollars?
5. Why does he think Sylvia can help him?
6. Why does she watch the toad so carefully?
7. Why does she leave the house before the sun comes up?
8. Why does she climb the tall pine tree?
9. What is the heron's secret?
10. Why can't she give the heron's secret away?

B. Close Reading: A Question of Time

Complete the sentences below by choosing **a**, **b**, or **c**. The first part of the sentence tells you something that happened in the story. The second part tells you when it happened.

1. Sylvia went to bring home the cow
   a. when the cow was ready to eat.
   b. just as it began to get dark.
   c. just after her grandmother was ready to eat.
2. Sylvia began to feel frightened
   a. at the same time that she heard the young man call out.
   b. after it began to get dark.
   c. when she lost the cow.
3. The young man wanted to stay with Sylvia and her grandmother

a. before they ate dinner.

b. while it began to get dark, but not after.

c. during the time that he hunted for birds.

4. They sat in the doorway

    a. as the moon came up.

    b. before it began to get dark.

    c. while the birds sang softly.

5. Sylvia decided to find the heron's nest

    a. as she was watching the toad.

    b. before it was dark.

    c. sometime during the night.

6. She had to climb the pine tree

    a. after the young man woke up.

    b. while it began to get dark.

    c. shortly before the sun came up.

7. She decided not to tell the young man where the heron lived

    a. after he said he would pay ten dollars.

    b. just before it began to get dark.

    c. because she saw how beautiful the heron was.

C. Discussion

1. What do you think about what the young man is doing? Is it work or play? This story was written about 100 years ago. Would you feel differently about him if he were hunting today? Why, or why not?

2. As you were reading the story, what did you think Sylvia would do? Do you think she should have helped the young man? Why, or why not?

3. The story says that Sylvia "couldn't understand why he killed the birds he liked so much." Explain her feelings for the birds, compared to the feelings of the young man. The young man tells her grandmother, "I stuff them to save them." In what way does he "save" the birds?

D. Vocabulary Practice

The underlined phrases in column B mean the same as a word or phrase in column A. Match the phrase in column **A** to the sentence with the same meaning in column **B**. Then write the new sentence.

Example:

A	**B**
getting darker	The woods were already <u>filled</u> <u>with</u> <u>shadows.</u>

<u>The</u> <u>woods</u> <u>were</u> <u>already</u> getting <u>darker.</u>

A	**B**
quite far away	**1.** She knows <u>every</u> <u>foot</u> <u>of</u> the woods.
faithfully	**2.** Sylvy, <u>step</u> <u>round</u> and set a plate for the gentleman.
lowered	**3.** You might <u>do</u> <u>better</u> if you went out to the road.
happily	**4.** This is the first time the world has <u>put</u> <u>out</u> <u>its</u> <u>hand</u> to her.
hurry up	**5.** The road is <u>a</u> <u>good</u> <u>ways</u> from here.
a lot about	**6.** Sylvia's face shone <u>like</u> <u>a</u> <u>star.</u>
have more success	**7.** She <u>dropped</u> her head like a broken flower.
tried to help	**8.** From the top of the tree Sylvia could see <u>the</u> <u>whole</u> <u>world.</u>
for miles	**9.** She would have loved him <u>as</u> <u>a</u> <u>dog</u> <u>loves.</u>

Write the new sentences here

1. _____

_____

2. _____

_____

3. _____

_____

4. _____

_____

5. _____

_____

6. _____

_____

7. _____

_____

8. _____

_____

9. _____

_____

E Word Forms

From the chart below, choose the form of the word that best fits the sentences below.

noun	adjective	adverb	verb
surprise	surprising	surprisingly	surprise
secret	secretive	secretly	secrete
hunter	hunted		hunt
shadow	shadowy		shadow
comfort	comfortable	comfortably	
stuffing	stuffed		stuff

1. (surprise) By the second day of his visit, Sylvia was _____ friendly with the young man.

2. (secret) Sylvia was a _____ child, perhaps because she was alone so much of the time.

3. (hunt) The young man was an unusual kind of _____.

4. (shadow) Neither Sylvia nor the cow were afraid of the _____ darkness. They were used to the woods.

5. (comfort) The three new-made friends were _____ with each other.

6. (stuff) What kind of _____ did the young man use inside his birds?

F. Language Activity: A Class Project on Wildlife Protection

In pairs or teams, investigate local environmental groups that work with wildlife protection, endangered species, and other environmental questions related to animals: animal rights, animal research, etc. Take notes, and make an oral report to the class.

G. Writing

Write a narrative (story) of your own. Choose one of the suggestions below:

1. You are Sylvia. You have told the young man where to find the heron. You go with him to hunt the bird. What happened then? How did you feel about it? What did you do?

2. You are the young man. When you see that Sylvia won't tell you where to find the bird, you try to persuade her to tell you. What happened then? Did

she tell you, finally? What did you do? How did you feel?

3. You are the grandmother. The day after the hunter left you found "Sylvy" in tears. Years later, you tell the story of what happened to Sylvia. Did she remain sad, or become happy again. Why? What became of her when she got older?